BISEXUALITY: THE BASICS

of related interest

BISEXUAL MEN EXIST
A Handbook for Bisexual, Pansexual and M-Spec Men
Vaneet Mehta
ISBN 978 1 78775 719 6
eISBN 978 1 78775 720 2

BI THE WAY
The Bisexual Guide to Life
Lois Shearing
ISBN 978 1 78775 290 0
eISBN 978 1 78775 291 7

IT AIN'T OVER TIL THE BISEXUAL SPEAKS
An Anthology of Bisexual Voices
Vaneet Mehta & Lois Shearing
ISBN 978 1 83997 195 2
eISBN 978 1 83997 196 9

MY CHILD TOLD ME THEY'RE TRANS... WHAT DO I DO?
A Q&A Guide for Parents of Trans Children
Brynn Tannehill
ISBN 978 1 83997 277 5
eISBN 978 1 83997 278 2

BISEXUALITY: THE BASICS

Your Q+A Guide to Coming Out, Dating, Parenting and Beyond

Lewis Oakley

Jessica Kingsley Publishers
London and Philadelphia

First published in Great Britain in 2024 by Jessica Kingsley Publishers
An imprint of John Murray Press

1

Content warning: This book contains mentions of biphobia.

A CIP catalogue record for this title is available from the
British Library and the Library of Congress

ISBN 978 1 83997 644 5
eISBN 978 1 83997 648 3

Printed and bound in Great Britain by TJ Books Limited

Jessica Kingsley Publishers' policy is to use papers that are natural,
renewable and recyclable products and made from wood grown in
sustainable forests. The logging and manufacturing processes are expected
to conform to the environmental regulations of the country of origin.

Jessica Kingsley Publishers
Carmelite House
50 Victoria Embankment
London EC4Y 0DZ

www.jkp.com

John Murray Press
Part of Hodder & Stoughton Limited
An Hachette UK Company

MIX
Paper from
responsible sources
FSC
www.fsc.org   FSC® C013056

To Laura,

This book is not just a collection of questions and answers; it's a testament to the unbelievable support, love and inspiration you have brought into my life. From the very beginning, you have stood by my side, embracing my bisexuality with an open heart.

You have not only given me the strength to be a proud and confident bisexual, but you have also been the best companion I could ask for in my journey as a bisexual advocate and activist. Whether I was participating in heated debates on TV or rushing off to give a speech, you were always there, caring for our three kids and providing me with the time and space I needed to make a difference in the world.

This book, these words, and the countless articles and discussions that came before it, all bear the mark of your love and support. You are my champion, my life partner and my greatest cheerleader. I am so grateful for your belief in me and for the strength and courage you've given me to pursue my passions.

Together, we've built a beautiful life filled with love, understanding and the freedom to be ourselves. None of this would have been possible without you by my side. You are the love of my life, my muse and my greatest source of inspiration.

Thank you for everything!

Lewis

Contents

About this Book

The Basics

In this chapter, we delve into the fundamental aspects of bisexuality, exploring the questions, concerns and experiences commonly encountered by people who identify as bisexual. We kick off by addressing the pivotal question – 'How do I know if I'm bisexual?' – moving all the way through to dealing with other people's perceptions of your sexuality. We also explore the link between bisexuality and pansexuality. This chapter is all about those early experiences, those times of exploration when putting labels on things might be the best thing or the worst thing.

Coming Out

The chapter 'Coming Out' explores the transformative

process of revealing your bisexuality to others, specifically focusing on the challenges, dilemmas and potential consequences that individuals may face when deciding to disclose their sexual orientation. This chapter offers guidance, personal anecdotes and strategies to help individuals navigate the intricacies of coming out.

Relationships

Relationships can be tricky for bisexual people. From your partner's perception of your bisexuality to your parents' confusion as to why you can't just 'choose' to be with someone of the opposite gender. In this chapter, we'll look at some of the unique pressures being bisexual can put on our relationships and how to handle them. We'll also explore the worries some bisexual people can have that it is better to stay in toxic relationships because no one else will accept their bisexuality. We also take a look at porn addiction and the urge to have biological children.

Sex

This chapter delves into the complexities around sex within the context of bisexuality. From fears to conversations, this chapter explores it all. Bisexuals can have such a broad spectrum of experience when it comes to sex. Maybe you've never had sex with someone of the same gender and you're worried about your first time.

Maybe you're scared of being honest with your healthcare provider about your recent sexual activity.

Mental Health

A chapter exploring the unique challenges and concerns related to mental well-being for individuals who identify as bisexual. From isolation to feeling inferior and everything in-between, we delve into the issues that can cause stress and discontent for bi people. Bisexuals are in largely unexplored territory, and it can feel as though you exist in an uncomfortable place between gay and straight culture. We also delve into the anxiety-inducing unpredictability bisexuality can bring, such as not even knowing the sex of your future partner, if having biological kids will be an option or if you can even get married where you live. Societal stereotypes can impact your self-worth; when you live in-between two societies, this can be magnified. Navigating that is what this chapter is all about.

The Community

A chapter exploring the challenges, nuances and complexities around bisexuality and the LGBTQ+ community. We also explore the LGBTQ+ community and its treatment of bi people and how it could do better to support us, and look at why a new bisexual entering your life isn't always a good thing.

Advice for Non-Bisexuals

In this chapter, we focus on the people who might turn to this book, not for themselves but to help them understand a bisexual person in their life. We explore the best ways they can help to support a bisexual person in their life and put some of their fears and worries to rest.

INTRODUCTION

Too many bisexuals feel alone. Few have other bisexual people to turn to and seek out advice. This can leave us in Groundhog Day – bisexuals doomed to repeat the same mistakes as their predecessors because no one was around to teach them the lessons. It's time to change that.

I've been actively involved in the bisexual space for years now, and in that time an almost countless number of bisexuals have written to me asking for advice. Bisexuals who felt they had nowhere else to turn but a guy from the internet whose article they read. I was successful because I managed to tease out the reality of being bisexual and explain it in an easy-to-access way that anyone, regardless of their sexuality, could understand. The frequency with which bisexuals were messaging me to ask for advice started to become unmanageable. This led me to launch an advice column – *Ask a Bi Dad* – which allowed the advice to be accessible to all bisexuals, not just the ones that emailed me.

What I learned over the years is that while the sex positions might be different, and the genders may vary, a lot of bisexuals struggle with the same issues. I've also been witness to bisexuals being able to flourish once provided with the insight to help them overcome these hurdles.

That's what I've pulled together for you all here – the ultimate bisexual FAQ. Each chapter provides answers to the most common issues we encounter across a range of topics, all designed to help you flourish as a bisexual. Although I'd love to guarantee every bisexual an active bi community, filled with people like them on hand to discuss their issues, cheer them on and have their back, it's not a promise that I can fulfil, which is why I've included all I've learned in the pages of this book. It's not a complete guide and it's not a magical shield that will stop you from getting hurt. It is a starting point – the bisexual basics if you will. From coming out, relationships, sex, through to mental health, the community and biphobia, the advice in this book is designed to arm you for some of the most common scenarios and trouble you're likely to run into.

THE BASICS

How do I know if I'm bisexual?

One of the biggest questions facing bi people can often be the simplest one of all: 'Am I bisexual?' For any LGBTQ+ person, knowing whether you are LGBTQ+ or not can be hard to determine, and it is especially hard when the world is filled with people who wish you were anything but.

When I was figuring out my sexuality, I was 19. I'd just moved to London and had been invited to some gay clubs. It was a world I hadn't experienced before: everyone was happy, proud of who they were. Men kissing men, women kissing women. I'd heard about it, of course, but nothing compared to being in a room like this and feeling all of that queer energy. It was an energy that said, 'If you have a problem with this, the joke is on you – we are having a great time.' It was only in this setting that I was able to feel safe enough to finally kiss a man – much to my own surprise.

This kicked off my search for my sexuality. Was I gay? Was I drunk? Bicurious? Bisexual? Trying to reach a conclusion on this was tricky – predominantly because I didn't know any other bisexual people. No one around me had had the same experience. What's more, there were so few bi people in the media or wider society to provide any comfort, context or inspiration.

Hopefully, the world is changing, but as many bi people will tell you, due to a long history of bi-erasure in the media and popular discourse, we never really saw bisexuality growing up. If you don't see something, or even know the word for it, it can be very hard to realize that you *are* it. We all look out to the wider society as we are growing up; we find things we connect with, and that helps us build our identity or at least a frame of reference. Sadly, for many of us, it can feel as if bisexuality is the world's best-kept secret.

It's not just a simple matter of seeing ourselves reflected in the media and society; it's also about how society views bisexuality and the impact that has on our own understanding of our attractions. As other bisexuals have pointed out to me, bi people are often defined by their attraction to men. If a woman is attracted to more than one gender, then people assume she is actually straight and is either experimenting or, worse, attention seeking. Similarly, if a man is attracted to more than one gender, they will say he is actually gay and lying about his attraction to women. This undermining of the bi experience is the reality of the world bisexuals have to exist in, and it makes it incredibly hard to understand your own attractions, particularly in those early days of discovery.

What can be really hard to deal with – but something you must be prepared for – is that these attitudes can actually come from other LGBTQ+ people, sometimes as a projection of their own insecurities or internalized homophobia. Some will even suggest that bisexuality is a phase you go through on your way to accepting that you're gay. This means that, all too often, bisexuals can feel that they are at the mercy of gay and straight advice, from people who have no experience of understanding bisexual feelings. In my case, I was surrounded by gay men, and many of them thought my attraction to men meant I was just like them – gay. Worse, many of them would tell me, 'Yeah, I used to say I was bisexual too.' When looking at all the evidence and opinions in the world around me, the conclusion was clear: I was gay.

And therein lay the first real clue in myself that I was bi. As unpleasant as it might be, often when the crowd is telling you one thing but something deep within you is rejecting it, the truth is about to be revealed. For me, it was people beginning to label me as gay that made me realize that wasn't right, that it didn't label my sexuality correctly.

If you are in the process of trying to understand your sexuality, one place you could try looking is in the past. Were there any indicators of being bisexual that you missed? For me, this was particularly true, but – in classic bi fashion – it can be complicated for a bisexual to understand.

Looking back, as a teenager, I understood I was attracted to women. All the other boys were too. We talked about it, we kissed girls – it was behaviour that was normal. Being surrounded by straight men and doing straight things made me believe I was straight. But what of my attraction to men? Turns out, it was there. I just misinterpreted it. Looking back, it is now obvious there were boys at school I was attracted to, but at the time I mistook this for wanting to be like them or wanting to be best friends with them. Really, I just wanted to kiss them.

The issue was that my brain didn't even think that was an option. I was straight, and society told me you could only be gay or straight, and I certainly wasn't gay. Had there been more bi people around or open in the media, maybe I would have figured it out sooner. As it was, I'd have to wait until I was 19 to begin the journey towards understanding my sexuality.

When trying to figure out if you are bisexual, another indicator could be the regularity of your attractions. A drunken same-sex kiss might be something different to a weekly/daily noticing of attractive people of differing genders. This approach isn't straightforward, though. Bi people can be more attracted to one gender than another; there's no rule to say you have to be equally attracted to men and women – it doesn't make you any less bi.

Ultimately, being bisexual is up to you. There is no magic formula, there is no sorting hat, there is no exam.

It's on you to listen to and understand your attractions to the point that you feel confident you've put the right label on them.

Everyone thinks I'm gay. Will people take me seriously as a bisexual?

This is a really common question, particularly among bisexual guys. I've met a lot of men over the years who publicly identify as gay, but who, upon meeting me, have disclosed that they are attracted to women as well as men. The problem for these men was that they felt no one would take them seriously if they came out as bisexual.

Men like this have often only ever dated men; perhaps the majority of their friends are also gay, and they feel that they are feminine presenting. All of this together can make someone feel that the idea they are attracted to women is just too unbelievable.

Coming out is never easy, and for men who have already come out as gay, to come out as bisexual years later is opening yourself up to hurt that you may have felt you'd already overcome.

For someone in this situation, it is a worry that people might not take you seriously. Your gay friends in particular may just dismiss it outright and make you the butt of every joke. The family that has come to accept you as gay might be confused as to why you've now 'suddenly discovered' your attraction towards women. And, perhaps most crucially, the women you're attracted to might not take you seriously as a potential love interest and see you as a *gay friend* at best.

Many people don't discuss the victimization bisexuals can suffer at the hands of other LGBTQ+ people. I've lost count of the number of gay men who have attacked my bisexuality over the years. People don't realize how much this can hurt – to be rejected by your own tribe. For a gay-identifying man coming out as bisexual, there is a real fear, not just of being mocked by your chosen family but of being kicked out of the 'gay tribe' altogether. 'You're no longer one of us.' 'We are bound by our sexuality and we no longer share that sexuality.' If you lost friends or family coming out as gay, you'll be all the more nervous that coming out again could cost you even more this time around.

Many bi women have also shared similar experiences with me. If, for example, they are in a same-sex relationship and want to come out, there is a real fear that the lesbian community will turn on them. That they won't be part of the tribe any more and they've 'chosen dick'. As with many of the issues we'll discuss later in this book, this situation certainly isn't the rule, and there are many LGBTQ+ people who aren't biphobic – but those aren't the ones you're reading an advice book for tips on how to handle.

So, ultimately, going back to the question, the sad and uninspiring answer is 'no'. It's highly probable that if you have spent many years identifying as gay/lesbian, it will take some people a while to understand and take you seriously. Unfortunately, some people might not ever fully accept your bisexual identity, and this is simply the time and culture we live in, when awareness and acceptance of bi people isn't widespread. In the future, a gay-identifying man coming out as bi might not be a *grab pearls and gasp* moment, but for now, bi people are unfortunately going to have to work harder than most to be taken seriously.

This is something I have had experience with, in the form of gay friends not believing in my bisexuality. I have often found that in these moments you must stay firm and reflect back what they are saying to you. How would they feel if you kept telling them they weren't really gay and they just hadn't found the right girl/boy yet? While I'm not encouraging you to be confrontational, it can help to make them walk a mile in your shoes.

It is also important to explain your thinking in a way people can follow. If you have good people around you, they really should understand and want to be supportive. It's not a crime for them to struggle to understand, so do your best to fill in the gaps for them and explain your reasons for coming out again. Something along the lines of:

When I was 16, I realized I liked men and thought that meant I was gay, so I just went with that. I didn't say anything, but I was always noticing that I had attractions to women even though everything about my life was gay. Now, I'm actually ready to admit what my 16-year-old self was too young to understand: that I am also attracted to women.

With regard to women not being interested in you because they think you are gay, all I can say is…welcome to the bisexual experience. There are many women out there who want to be with the kind of man society deems as 'manly' – someone rugged, strong, straight…one who has never had a dick in his mouth. But, in truth, the majority of bisexuals are in opposite-sex relationships. That means there are also plenty of women out there who don't enforce toxic standards of masculinity and would be more than open to dating a bi man.

Oftentimes, it's bi men themselves who don't believe this. So often we struggle with the feeling of inadequacy. We might think, 'This is a woman who's only ever dated straight men; there is no way she'd be interested in someone as feminine as me. Someone who's 27 and never even had sex with a woman. At worst, she'll see me as gay; at best, she'll see me as a virgin.'

It's *take your breath away* anxiety levels. But just go for it! As bisexuals, we need to get better at not ruling ourselves out – the world is already doing that for us. If you're attracted to someone, wait for them to tell you they aren't interested; don't just assume it and stay inside your little inadequate box.

You are not just your sexuality; you're you and you have a lot of unique things to offer. Be the best salesperson you can be – the product you are selling is you, after all. And as you've been working on you since day one, I'd hope you're relatively happy with the product. Don't let your bisexuality be a handicap. I've met a lot of men over the years who used the ambiguity around their sexuality to their advantage, seeming to enjoy creating a mystery that intrigued people to want to know more.

Ultimately, coming out as gay makes people feel as though they've overcome a hurdle. They find support in knowing that the people who stayed and accepted them are there for life. Coming out again feels like you're risking all that again. Will you be accepted again? Will those around you accept that you aren't gay but bi? The truth is, if people around you can't accept that you are bi, then you need to reassess their position in your life and in your heart. Your bisexuality shouldn't matter; it is who you are, and you'll be a more confident version of yourself knowing that those you care about embrace you and cheer you on as a bisexual.

How do I prove to the haters that I'm not secretly gay?

In a world that often assumes bisexual men are secretly gay, it can be a common desire to want to prove that you aren't gay.

The truth is, it's not a healthy place to be: to want to prove your sexuality to someone. Your sexuality isn't a court case or a parking ticket where you need to submit evidence and wait for a jury to reach a verdict. It is yours, it's true, and other people's opinions aren't going to change it.

That's easy for someone to say, but much harder when

you are feeling this immense social pressure to prove that you aren't gay.

Clearly, the most obvious way to prove you aren't gay is to do something sexual with a woman. This is called using someone. Pushing to be seen to date or have sex with women to set the record straight is no way to handle this situation. It is completely disrespectful to the woman and truly a sign that you are letting others' negative interpretations drive bad behaviour in yourself.

What I have found effective over the years is actually leaning into your gay experience. The truth is, as a bisexual you're not embarrassed by your attraction towards men. If you were gay, you'd gladly come out as gay.

Hammering home that point can be a game changer. When people have challenged me and suggested I'm secretly gay, I usually start listing off all the gay things I've done. I'm not embarrassed about my history with men; I'm bloody proud of it. I had a great time and met a lot of heartbreakers, and even today, we're so blessed to live in a world with so many sexy men walking around all over the place. My attractions towards men are a blessing – I'm not trying to cover them up with the bi label.

I feel that there is a darker side to these comments. When someone implies that you're gay, they're actually accusing you of internalized homophobia. They think you're embarrassed and scared, and that on some level you think being gay is wrong – that you're using bisexuality as a cover to make you appear less gay. Affirming your desire for men, proclaiming your comfortableness in your sexuality and talking about your attraction to men will, nine times out of ten, call their bluff. Of course, there's a flipside to this and you could just as easily ask, 'How do I prove to the haters that I'm not straight?' Bisexual people are often defined by their attraction to men, so while bisexual men are often assumed to be gay, bisexual women are often assumed to be straight. And my advice to bi women would be the same. Be open about your gay experiences and be proud of who you are. And remember, you don't have to prove yourself to anyone.

How do I make sure the world doesn't just see me as bisexual?

Many bisexuals report not being able to be open enough about their sexuality, and many spend time trying to find ways to display it as loudly as possible. For some bisexuals, though, the opposite is true. They aren't embarrassed by their sexuality, but they do worry that people won't be able to see past it.

They fear that after coming out, people will always see them as 'the bi one'. Biphobia also factors into this: what if people discriminate against you because of your bisexuality?

One example of this could be in a work setting. You have a good relationship with colleagues but you fear coming out might impact those relationships. What if colleagues of the opposite sex see you differently after coming out and you just sense it's changed the way they see you? On the other hand, what if your company think it's fabulous and all of a sudden put you in charge of their LGBTQ+ drive and expect you to be a voice for bi people in the company?

Other bisexuals may just not see what the big deal is. They are a poet or good at playing darts, and that's what they want people to see when they think of them. Not their sexuality. Balancing this desire for your sexuality to not be a 'big deal' with not wanting to be closeted can be tricky.

If you do feel this way, one of the best things you can do is realize that if being seen as not just a bisexual is your desire, it's on you to make it your reality. It's all about PR. You only have to come out to someone once; you can then spend the rest of your time with them discussing all the elements of your personality that you want to be defined by. Take them to your poetry slam night, write a verse in their birthday card; whatever it is that you want to be defined by will shine through.

I can't lie: for some people, your sexuality might be a 'thing', but it will be hard to keep thinking about it if all your interactions with them are regarding other things. Defining yourself by your passions, interests and accomplishments will ensure they see you as more than just a bisexual.

It's also important that you have clear boundaries. If people turn to you as their bisexual resource and you don't like it, make it clear to them that you're not the arbiter of bisexuality. Just because you are bisexual doesn't mean you're a bi-spokesperson. You don't have all the answers and don't care to get into it. If your sexuality comes up in conversations at a rate you aren't comfortable with, tell them you're bored of talking about it and move on.

While there is nothing wrong with not wanting to be labelled and put in a box, it is important that you also accept that there is nothing wrong with being 'the bi one' – it's a badge you should wear with pride.

Does kissing someone of the same sex when I get drunk really make me bisexual?

A common scenario I've seen play out over the years is people discovering their bisexuality after having a drink.

I've discovered that it is common for bisexuals to be much older when they realize their sexuality. In my case, I grew up believing I was straight. I was attracted to women, and attraction to women was what the other boys talked about. For many gay men, when the other boys start discussing their attraction to women, it often forces them to confront why they don't feel the same (and vice versa for gay women). Although they might not fully understand their same-sex attraction, gay men and women will likely have a sense early on of not conforming to the norm.

Yet, as always, bisexuals can blend in, even with themselves. For me, it wasn't until I was 19, drunk and in a gay club that my attractions to men could finally manifest. It wasn't that I'd ever tried to hide them; I genuinely didn't know they were there.

Many bisexuals have told me the same thing: that their

sexual realization happened later in life, in a situation where alcohol had lowered their inhibitions and something that felt strangely natural happened.

However, this isn't the case for everyone. So, how do you really know if kissing someone of the same sex when you're drunk is actually a sign of bisexuality or just a good time?

For me, the biggest indicator would be its frequency. I didn't just kiss a boy and like it once; it became a regular thing. Maybe, on some level, I needed the courage alcohol can provide as I opened the scary door to this new side of myself.

Equally, you don't have to be having same-sex smooches in the club every Friday. It might have only happened once. But if it's stuck in your mind and is something you keep thinking about, it's probably a sign that it meant more to you than just a tipsy thing that happened once.

Like it or not, alcohol can give some bisexuals the confidence to act on their feelings for the first time. I would go as far as to suggest that coming out later in life is slightly harder than doing it in your teen years. As an adult, you can often feel established as straight, and smashing that perception to everyone you know in pursuit of a sexuality that you don't quite yet fully understand is completely terrifying.

That's why I think that the alcohol scenario is a common one. Bars and clubs lend themselves to anonymity. When people don't know you, you can kiss someone and disappear; it won't stay on your record forever. It feels like a safe place to test the bisexual waters. Coming out as a bisexual to a stranger you meet at a bar carries minimal risk. If they have a bad reaction, you don't have to see them ever again.

For all its faults, alcohol can provide some people with the courage their sober self just wouldn't muster. Obviously, this question does come with a substance warning, and it should noted that there have been a few studies which conclude that bisexuals have disproportionate levels of substance abuse (Tobkes and Davidson, 2017).

You don't want to get into the habit of needing alcohol to access your bisexuality. Although it might play a role at the beginning of some bisexual journeys, it's not a long-term strategy.

How do I know if I'm bicurious or bisexual?

Having an attraction to more than one gender can be confusing, especially when you are young. I've been told many stories of people who experimented in their younger years but are now happily straight or gay.

It doesn't always mean that you're bisexual. Yet that can be hard to determine, particularly in a world where many feel that once you go queer, there is no going back. That kissing someone of the same gender is a solidifying experience, carved in stone, that will be with you forever.

The first thing to do when approaching this question is to change the way you think. Kissing someone shouldn't be a big deal – as long as they are consenting. As with most things bisexual, try to take the gender out of it. If you think someone is hot, if there's chemistry, would you see kissing them as a life-changing moment that you can never escape? Or just something fun that happened in the moment? It might lead somewhere; it might not. It could end up as a funny story or you could completely forget it even happened.

This is the kind of attitude you need to have when exploring your sexuality: it's not life-defining unless you want it to be.

When it comes to actually knowing if you're bi or just a little curious, the correct answer is: *only you will know*. But this is an advice book, so there are a few signs I can highlight to help guide your self-discovery.

It really comes down to frequency and variation. How frequently are you having the urge to be intimate in some way with someone of the same gender? Was it just the one time or has it happened a few times? Have your attractions been to multiple people or was it one specific person?

A basic rule would be the higher the frequency of attraction and the greater number of different people your attractions lead you to, the greater the chance you're bisexual and not bicurious.

Some people have an issue with the word 'bicurious', but I'm a big fan. I spent quite a while telling myself I was bicurious. It was a term that took the pressure off. It meant that I didn't have to 'make a decision' or identify a particular way. It gave me the ambiguity and the freedom to really explore my attractions, who I wanted to kiss, who I wanted to take home, and to really figure out what I enjoyed.

If you find yourself drawn to the label, go for it! It's empowering – and don't let anyone tell you otherwise. You're actually doing bisexuals a favour as it helps to reduce the stigma around bisexuality being a phase. The more people who use the word 'bicurious' when they are exploring their sexuality, the fewer people will associate the word 'bisexuality' with an exploratory phase.

Am I bisexual or pansexual?

I was hesitant about putting this question in the book. The debate over what is bisexual and what is pansexual seems to be able to turn rather toxic astoundingly quickly. I really don't want us to be wasting good time fighting each other on differences in definitions and labels when there is clearly far more that unites us than divides us.

The questions about what is bisexual and what is pansexual have increased over the years. Let me start this question by saying that I'm not the arbiter of who gets to use what label. You need to decide for yourself which one you identify with more.

I'm not going to give you the Google definitions of these two sexualities; I trust you to go and do that on your own. I also want to make clear that I'm not trying to offend anyone if you feel differently; I'm just telling my truth from my experience.

At the heart of this issue, bisexuality is defined as an

attraction to more than one sex or gender, whereas pansexuality is defined as an attraction not defined by sex or gender. So what does that mean? If both sexualities are attracted to more than one gender, isn't it just the same thing? The subtle difference is in the concept that pansexuals experience attraction to any sex/gender, whereas bisexuals might have a few favourites.

Again, while I'm not the arbiter of this issue, this is my book and it might help some people out there for me to explain it in the terms that I understand. For me, bisexuality means that gender and sex play a role in the attraction. For a pansexual person, gender or sex is inconsequential; they are attracted to the person. Not to be confused with not finding their partner sexuality attractive.

For me, the gender of the person plays a part in my attraction to them. Seeing a very feminine woman or a very masculine man happens to be sexy to me for some reason. If their personality were switched into another body of a different sex, would I still find them as attractive? I'm not sure, and that's why I think the bi label applies to me, because it's not just the soul of the person I find hot, but how they display their gender identity is also hot.

That's just the musings of one mad bisexual. You're going to have to do the work yourself and identify the label that works for you. Maybe, like me, you'll struggle to articulate why one label seems to work over the other, and that's okay too.

Before we move on from this subject, we should explore the origins of the words: pan being Greek for all and bi being Greek for two. Typically, this has been interpreted as pansexuals being attracted to all people – which isn't correct – and bi people being seen as attracted to cis men and women – which is exclusionary to all other gender identities, and also not correct. The origins of these words are really in the past, and the words have evolved in their meaning, as words tend to do.

I'm bisexual but does that mean I have to be part of a movement?

An interesting thing I've run into in more recent years is the debate about whether simply being LGBTQ+ means that you're automatically enrolled into the queer movement and instantly made a warrior for the cause.

I've known many bisexuals (and gay men and lesbians) that have rejected the calling, preferring not to see themselves as part of a community or a movement. As far as they are concerned, their sexuality is a matter-of-fact issue; it doesn't mean they have to support certain ideologies, vote a particular way or give the LGBTQ+ community a second of their time.

Each to their own, and I can certainly see both sides here. In truth, the idea of belonging to a big queer family with important work to do in the world can be daunting.

In my experience, the unfortunate reality is that, like it or not, at the very least, you'll become an ambassador for the cause. The wider culture that we exist in has an issue with bisexuality, no matter how progressive it professes to be. You are going to run into people who see your sexuality as a negative thing, people who have preconceived notions about who you are. You'll have no choice but to defend yourself, to set the record straight.

And, support it or not, the LGBTQ+ movement is a vehicle designed to give you an easier life. That doesn't mean you have to support everything it says. Lord knows, no one has been more critical of the LGBTQ+ movement and its lacklustre efforts to support bi people than me. I have found, however, that it's far better to address the 'movement' and campaign for it to do a better job than pretend it doesn't exist altogether.

You have to find a way to exist within the movement that's right for you. You don't have to attend a single Pride event, you don't need to own a bi flag and you don't need to engage in bisexual culture. Equally, you could run your local LGBTQ+ group and take up some campaigning. It's really up to each individual and you shouldn't feel pressure.

It's also true that your bisexuality has no real impact on your politics. There are plenty of bisexual conservatives, just as there are plenty of bi liberals. Being bi doesn't necessarily mean you have to have more of a focus on equality.

One unique attitude I've seen from some bisexuals is actually that of being 'anti-woke'. These are bisexuals who feel betrayed and let down by the left-leaning movements. They feel that they often run into people who claim to be kind and compassionate – but not when it comes to bi-sexuals. In particular, I've seen the underwhelming efforts of the LGBTQ+ movement towards the bi community turn bisexual people away from liberal-leaning ideology. Ultimately, they feel let down and hurt. It's not to say that they agree with the right; they just seem to focus more on the hypocrisy of the left. Some bisexuals have the sense that it's always about someone else's equality. I'd like to see this improve over the coming years, but that will only happen if people who profess to be there for minorities can tangibly prove how they have achieved this for bi people.

As a bisexual, you don't need to be part of a movement. Being bi will give you a unique perspective on the wider issues in society that usually guarantees you to be a critical thinker.

Why is it still taboo to talk about bisexuality?

I often find bisexuality is a topic that makes a lot of people uncomfortable. Despite what some would have you believe, this isn't just a certain section of people; I've met many progressives who have their heads filled with as many biphobic tropes as anyone. Biphobia – or bi-ignorance as I sometimes call it – seems to transcend political leanings, and even sexualities, with the LGBTQ+ community not immune from having biphobic voices among its ranks.

But why? What's the problem?

In my opinion, there are a few factors. The first is that it 'affects them where they live' to steal a phrase. What a lesbian gets up to, for example, doesn't affect a straight man because they can't date. A bi person, on the other hand, has the potential to be romantically/sexually interested in a straight person. This means that the straight person has to consider if they would date somebody bi, and usually a defence mechanism kicks in where they repeat all of the biphobic information they've absorbed. All of a sudden, a bi person isn't just a concept they can support in the abstract; it's something they have to scrutinize to protect their heart.

Another uncomfortable element is that the word 'bisexual' contains the word 'sex' – in contrast to the labels 'gay' and 'lesbian', which are used much more commonly than 'homosexual'. Some feel that this makes bi people seem provocative, and that's partly why some people respond negatively towards us. Basically, we are sex mad and trying to get them in our beds. If we dig a little deeper into this theory, we have to understand that for bisexuals in relationships, being open with your partner about your attraction to multiple genders can be misinterpreted – you might be seen as more of a flight risk or as having a roving eye. We find ourselves at an uncomfortable intersection in the culture – if we don't talk about our sexuality, then perceptions aren't going to change. People will view us as straight or gay, completely defined by our partners, our bisexuality won't be visible and it will continue to be viewed as a phase. On the other hand, if we do talk about our sexuality, it can be seen as us being more inclined to cheating.

Looking at this from another perspective, if a married straight man went around talking about how much he finds women attractive and explaining what it is about certain women that catches his eye, people would see this as being disrespectful to his wife and conclude he is at risk of being unfaithful. This logic is then applied to bisexuals, and it makes people uneasy because they aren't used to couples discussing their attractions outside of their partners. The reality, of course, is that this is just a societal hang-up. We all know that hormones don't disappear when you get into a relationship; it doesn't mean you're going to cheat – it's just nature. Unfortunately, that reality makes a lot of people uncomfortable.

The final reason is that, unfortunately, many people honestly believe that bisexuality is a phase: they think bi women are really straight and just looking for fun/ attention, and they think bi men are secretly gay and lying to themselves. If you truly believe this, then when someone tells you that they are bi, you think they are lying to you. If you think someone is lying to you, it makes you distrust them; it makes you suspicious and prevents you from bonding. We are undeservedly held back by this. As long as people think that bisexuality is a phase, they won't trust us. At best, they'll think we don't understand ourselves, which is demeaning to bi people and makes us not like them.

Bisexuality remains taboo for a lot of people; it makes them uncomfortable. But part of being out and walking with pride is about holding people to account and not letting them get away with treating us badly because we make them uncomfortable. Make sure you lead these discussions if they come up. Biphobia and bi-ignorance are not evolving arguments; no one is coming up with any new points on why bisexuality doesn't exist, which means, at a certain point, you'll have heard it all. I make sure I have about three points to say to every biphobic point I've ever heard. If someone says to me, 'Yeah, but bisexuals choose to be gay or straight eventually', they are going down. I've prepared for this; no one is going to have anything more thought-out to say when it comes to bisexuality than I do (barring other bi people). You have to have confidence that while bisexuality makes some uncomfortable, we are here to demystify it and prove to them, whether argumentatively or kindly, that their negative assumptions are wrong.

Eventually, with enough bisexuals being unapologetic about who they are, we'll turn the tide and make sure it's less taboo to talk about.

Why is there never any good bisexual merch?

It is a complete paradox that in a world where bisexuals struggle to be seen that there isn't more bisexual merchandise on offer. A gay person needs only to hold their partner's hand in public to be visible for their sexuality. Unfortunately, should a bi person hold their partner's hand, they'll be seen as either gay or straight. We are a visual species, and bisexuals are wrongly defined by their partners. Having a bisexual T-shirt, a badge or some trainers would be a great way to signal their sexuality to those passing by.

Some may view this as a superficial issue. Why do you care if strangers on the street know if you're bisexual or not? The reality is that bisexuality has an invisibility problem. If people can't see it, they don't believe it exists. If they don't believe it exists, then they will be ignorant of it, they won't invest resources in it and the issue won't move forward. For bisexuals, at this particular point in history, being visible is critical to our liberation and improving the world for the next generation of bisexuals. It's also nice for us bisexuals who happen to be settled in relationships to feel as though we are in some way helping the cause, and smashing the idea that we 'turned' gay or straight.

So, why is there an endless selection of gay and lesbian merchandise and so little on offer for the bisexuals? I think in part it's a chicken-and-egg situation. Companies don't see bisexuals and so they don't create products for them. There are some fabulous bisexuals out there with Etsy stores and the like trying to change this, but we really need big companies to help and, critically, to give us a range of options. Not every bisexual is going to be down for the loud colours of the Pride or bisexual flag – won't someone spare a thought for the bisexual goths? I actually took to making my own bisexual merchandise, creating T-shirts that were more my style, so that I felt comfortable wearing them.

If more bisexuals put pressure on brands and start asking, 'Where are the bisexual options?' we might just be able to influence the outcomes on this issue. What's more, if people start seeing there is a profit to be made from the 'bisexual bitcoin', that consumerist system may just help bisexuals become more visible.

What are the problems facing bisexuals?

Despite making up the majority of the LGB population, bisexual-specific issues remain largely unexamined. As you might expect, if things are unexamined, then it's unlikely you're going to be able to improve them.

As a bi person, I've actually found it empowering to know some of the issues you're most likely to encounter, because this helps you to contextualize your experience. Knowing you've fallen into a pothole that captures many bisexuals can ease the blame we place on ourselves but also hopefully help us avoid the pothole altogether.

For bi men, one of the biggest issues I've come across is that many women tend not to want to date them. In a survey of over 1000 women, 63 per cent of women said they wouldn't date a man who's had sex with another man (Tsoulis-Reay, 2016). Interestingly, this isn't just men who identify as bi. This includes all men who've experimented with another man, even if it only happened once. Similarly, a YouGov poll identified that just 28 per cent of women say they would be comfortable with the idea of a bisexual partner (Ballard, 2019). Finally, a 2018 study published in the *Journal of Bisexuality* concluded that straight women perceive bi men as being less romantically and sexually attractive than straight men. As a result, straight women were less likely to date or have sex with a bi guy. Bi men were also perceived as being significantly more feminine than straight men (Gleason, Vencill and Sprankle, 2018).

Although these pieces of research are by no means exhaustive (bisexuality is an under-researched area!), they do point to a worrying trend, confirming what many bi men see in their day-to-day dating experiences – that a lot of women appear to have a no-tolerance attitude to men who aren't 100 per cent straight. As one bisexual put it to me, if a large majority of women don't want to date bi men, doesn't coming out as bi really mean you're coming out as gay by default?

From my observations, the fear that women will reject them is one of the biggest factors in keeping bi men closeted. Many feel that it's better to take their chances and say nothing. Feeling that there is a part of you that you need to hide because it makes you so unattractive is a very unhealthy way to live. Sadly, it's not much better when it comes to bi men seeking relationships with gay men. A lot of bi men have experienced gay men willing to sleep with them, or even date them, but not fully accept them as bi. Being in a relationship with someone who discredits or disbelieves your sexual orientation is equally as damaging as being rejected altogether.

Things are just as bleak on the bi female side. Bi women in particular report being perceived as hypersexualized – the bringer of men's fantasies – for they allow a man to have sex with two women at once. This hypersexualization is dangerous, with figures showing that sexual violence is also more common against bisexual women than it is straight women or lesbians. Between 2015 and 2017, Office for National Statistics (ONS) figures show 11 per cent of bi women reported abuse by their partner, compared with 8 per cent of lesbians and 6 per cent of straight women (Glass, 2018).

Many bi women have also told me that lesbians can be suspicious of them, not seeing them as 'queer enough'. Some have even said that they are seen as traitors for their ability to find both men and women attractive. They are, in short, perceived as having bisexual privilege – not really suffering enough to be part of the club.

Bisexuals are in a unique situation because many date outside of their sexual orientation: a bi man can date straight women, gay men and other bi people. This means we have to deal with people romantically who don't share our sexuality. Could you imagine if coming out as gay made you less attractive to gay men? It just wouldn't happen, but for bi people coming out, the worry is that your very sexuality makes you less attractive to the vast majority of people you're attracted to.

This brings us nicely on to the issue of mental health. Mental health is hard to assess when it comes to bi people, particularly because of the way in which research is conducted. Some studies amalgamate the entire LGBTQ+ community, and this can make it tricky for bisexual people to understand the findings as different issues may be impacting the mental health of a bi woman compared with, say, a gay man. Similarly, some studies don't take into account the role gender plays in mental health issues.

That said, there are some studies out there that I think are reputable and will help you to contextualize the greater risks you might experience as a bi person:

The ONS has found that bisexual people are nearly 80 per cent more likely to report feeling anxious than the average person, with around one-third reporting high levels of anxiety. Bisexual people were also 40 per cent more likely to describe themselves as unhappy (Jackman, 2017).

The 'Who I Am' study, conducted by La Trobe University, questioned more than 2600 bisexual people across Australia, finding that those who perceive their sexuality to be bad or wrong have poor mental health. More than 60 per cent of respondents had high or very high current psychological distress. The study also revealed that 40 per cent reported having had depression in the past (La Trobe University, 2019).

When it comes to suicide, the Human Rights Campaign concluded that one in three bisexual men has considered or attempted suicide, with bi youths having a higher incidence of suicidal thoughts and suicide attempts than gay and lesbian youth (Kristal, 2017).

Of course, no list could be exhaustive when it comes to the issues facing bisexual people. Throughout the rest of this book, you'll receive a detailed overview of many issues that impact bi people and, hopefully, a few ideas on how to deal with them.

COMING OUT

Coming out is one of the hardest rites of passage for any queer person. For bisexuals, this comes with unique struggles. I've pulled together some of the most common questions on the topic of coming out to explore, delving into the details of why someone might ask the question, as well as offering advice for practical ways forward.

How do I come out to my family?

Coming out to family can be one of the most terrifying things a bisexual can do. It opens you up to the possibility of rejection and judgement from those who have known you all your life.

When we think of coming out, we tend to think about people in their teens – young people discovering their sexuality and being honest with their relatives. In this situation, there is so much on the line – the roof over your head for one. If your parents don't accept your sexuality and want you out, how will you cope? Just as stressful is not being rejected but at the same time not being understood – having to continue living where you are but dealing with judgement and ignorant comments as part of your daily life.

Less often, we think of people in their 30s, 40s or even older. This comes with just as many hurdles. Some may argue it's slightly easier because the majority have financial independence. But family is just as significant at any age. It's also important to remember that as we talk about the families of older bisexuals, we can also be talking about their children – kids scared and upset, wondering what this revelation means and how their lives will change.

For many families, culture and religion can play a huge role. Many times, bisexuals will delay coming out because they can predict that the outcome in their religion or culture will not be favourable.

The truth is, whether you are young, old, religious or agnostic, coming out to your family boils down to one thing. Fear. The fear of rejection. The fear of things changing. The fear of being labelled.

So, what's the best way to move forward? When is the best time to come out? And how do you approach the subject?

In my experience, and drawing on all I've learned from other people, *you'll know when the right time is*. It sounds like cliché, but it's the truth. One day, your bisexuality being part of your identity will click. It will build to the point that it's non-negotiable. It will give you the strength to handle the possibility of rejection because you're no longer willing to play a straight character to please others. I'm sure you will have put up with difficult times and outright nonsense from your family over the years, but accepting you becoming an authentic and open version of yourself is really the least they can do.

For the first time, you'll know that they aren't going to be able to catch you out or even change your mind. That nothing they can say is going to be a magic spell to turn you straight. That you're in control, you're laying out the facts, and they are just the audience in your bisexual story – they aren't steering this ship.

I spent years planning to come out and backing out every time. It's only looking back years later that I realize why I backed out all those times. It was simply because, even though on paper I was ready to come out, I hadn't truly accepted my sexuality. A small part of me still felt it was wrong or different. As soon as it clicked, and I not only accepted myself but was proud and happy to be bisexual, I finally had the strength to come out. Because, no matter what, I'm the toughest critic of myself, and if I think this is a good thing, then nothing anyone else can say will make me doubt myself.

What's important to remember is that your family has always had a bisexual relative. All that's changing is now they will know about it. Last Christmas, at weddings and birthdays, you were there, and you were bisexual. What did it really change for them? Nothing. So, knowing that you're bisexual doesn't change anything and shouldn't impact on how they feel about you. Sometimes they might just need reminding of that.

Of course, this story doesn't always have a happy ending. Sometimes coming out is disastrous, damaging and, in some circumstances, dangerous. I can't, in good conscience, say that it's better for everyone to be out of the closet. What I can say is that it should be. And, if possible, living your true self, not having to hide things from those you love, is a much healthier and happier existence.

I feel that a good way to judge this situation is to consider *respect*. Do you deserve the respect to be accepted? You do have to ask yourself, if your family have an issue with your sexuality, if they judge or reject you because of it, are they really the people you want in your life? Can you live with the love they have for you being conditional? Especially when that condition is that you must be straight – something you are incapable of being? Losing family members is a nuclear option, no question, but it can't be an option off the table, otherwise you're fighting with one hand behind your back.

Of course, coming out is only step one. Now for all their questions. Are you really gay? Can't you just choose women/men? What woman/man is going to want to be with you? Does this mean you and mommy/daddy don't love each other any more? The final component in choosing to come out to your family is taking some time to think about what their follow-up questions could be. Luckily, you have this book.

Is it worth coming out to my family?

One perspective that I've often heard from bisexual people is that there is no point in coming out and risking upset to their family if they might end up with someone of the opposite gender anyway.

It's a unique situation. A gay man knows that he must come out unless he is planning to keep his partner a secret from his family. For bi people, depending on the gender of their partner, they could appear straight to their family.

This idea becomes a delaying tactic, with some bi people reasoning there is no need to upset their family yet and choosing to wait until they settle down with a partner to make a call on coming out.

In truth, the fact that you might end up with someone of the opposite gender is beside the point. Coming out is about allowing those who love you to know the real you and for you to know that you are accepted and loved. If you're looking for a hack or a cheat to get around it, it means that you've not really accepted your sexuality.

It means you're keeping your family at arm's length, not letting them into a big part of your life. This approach means that you don't come out at all, depending on the gender of the person you end up with. That means you can't draw on your family's advice and support throughout your dating journey. It also means always keeping a secret if you do end up in a straight-facing relationship.

This approach also puts pressure on you and a potential partner. In the back of your mind, you'll be hoping to end up with someone of the opposite gender, as a way to avoid an uncomfortable situation. Whether you admit it or not, it will play a factor in your decision making and perhaps even cause anxiety around a partner if they happen to be the same sex as you.

It's also not great for this pressure to be on a same-sex partner. They might wonder why you aren't out to your family and why they need to be kept a secret *until you're sure they are the one*. They also might feel very nervous for you when you do decide to tell your family and feel on some level that it's their fault. If you had found a nice opposite-sex partner instead of them, you wouldn't be going through this pain.

You also have to consider your family in this situation: to find out you're bi and that you already have a secret partner is a lot to take in all at once. They could feel extreme sadness that you felt the need to keep it all a secret. Equally, they could think that your new partner is to blame and that they've turned you bi.

As tempting as it might be and as difficult as it is to come out, my advice would be not to let the gender of your partner be the deciding factor on if you share your true identity with the family you love.

Should I be out on dating profiles?

There are pros and cons to being out on dating apps and, more widely, being out before a first date. Some may choose to remain closeted until the relationship is official, or include their coming out in that conversation around becoming an official couple.

I've gone back and forth on this issue, and there honestly isn't a correct answer. You have to do what is right for you. If you have your sexuality in your dating profile, then, as a bi woman, you might get some creepy men who will have ridiculous views about what it means for their sex lives. You could face unwanted attention and even fetishization, with many hoping you'll be up for threesomes. Mentioning your bisexuality upfront may also unintentionally lead to an overemphasis on your sexuality rather than other aspects of your personality or interests. There are also many lesbians and straight men who might reject you outright on the basis of your sexuality. As a bi man, both the previously mentioned research and anecdotal evidence from other bi men has suggested that there are straight women who will not want to connect with you if they know you're bi. Ultimately, being bi on a dating profile will reduce your dating pool. Those are the cards we've been dealt by society, and I don't think anyone can judge us for whichever way we decide to manage the situation.

A lot of bi men I know have chosen to keep their sexuality a secret from straight women until it looks like the relationship is solidifying. Although this tactic might not end happily, if you know that your sexuality is going to be a deal breaker for a lot of women, then hiding it until they get to know you better seems like a sensible strategy. They might be put off initially by the thought of a bi man, but after three weeks of dating, sex and a genuine connection, would it still be a deal breaker?

Some bisexuals have less tolerance than that and think 'to hell' with anyone that has an issue with bisexuality. More power to this approach!

Whatever you choose, don't let anyone judge you and don't judge yourself. We didn't ask for this situation, and we are just trying to make the best decisions we can.

What's the best way to let my current partner know I'm bisexual?

If you're a bisexual who has chosen to keep your sexuality secret until your relationship is confirmed as exclusive, the thought of coming out can be daunting.

My first piece of advice here would be to not wait too long before having the conversation, no matter how anxiety-inducing it is. I'd say it should be around the time you decide to 'make it official', and it could even be part of that discussion.

You could explain, 'I'd really like to make this official, but there is something about myself that I haven't shared yet, and I wanted to get it on the table before I ask you if you'd like to become my partner.'

Other people prefer not to make a big deal of it, such as when you're curled up watching a film together and you remark on someone of the same gender being attractive – basically, trying to pass off your coming out as banter.

There are millions of ways to come out – some people

even use placards and a spreadsheet. You have to find which one is most natural for you. You also need to be ready to answer questions. If they've never dated a bisexual before, it's only natural that they'll want to understand what having a bi partner means and what a relationship would look like. Some questions you might be asked include:

◆ Have you had sex with men/women before?

◆ Are you sure you aren't gay?

◆ Would you want an open relationship?

◆ Will I be enough for you?

◆ How do you know you won't miss gay sex eventually?

Yes, there might be some basic questions in there. Just remember, you're in this situation because you really like this person, so try not to get too mad if something silly falls out of their mouth. One report has found that 89 per cent of young people report learning nothing about bisexuality issues at school. Blame the education system that you're in this situation; you're having to be the teacher (Metro Charity, 2017).

Is it too late to let my wife know I'm bisexual?

Well, here we are. This is the big one. In six years of writing and being an activist on bisexuality, the 'How do I come out to my wife?' question has been by far the most commonly asked. It's by far the trickiest to get right and its very existence is one of the saddest realities of bisexuality – how did we end up here?

Let's start with how we ended up here. A lot of straight women tend to not want to date bisexual men. So that you're clear this is based on fact and not me stereotyping, here is all the research on the topic:

- In a survey of more than 1000 women, conducted by *Glamour* in 2016, 63 per cent of women said they wouldn't date a man who's had sex with another man (Tsoulis-Reay, 2016). (This isn't just men who identify as bi, but includes all men who've experimented with another man, even if it only happened once!)

- In 2019, a YouGov poll found that just 28 per cent of women say they would be comfortable with the idea of a bisexual partner (Ballard, 2019).

- A study published in the *Journal of Bisexuality* concluded that straight women perceive bi men as being less romantically and sexually attractive than straight men. As a result, straight women were less likely to date or have sex with a bi guy. Bi men were also perceived as being significantly more feminine than straight men (Gleason *et al.*, 2018).

- A study out of Australia found that 44 per cent of Australians wouldn't date someone who is bisexual (Perrie, 2021).

Of course, women don't have a responsibility to find bisexual men attractive. If there are women who say they won't date a bi man because they think he is secretly gay or a cheating risk, that is clearly misinformed stigma and wrong. But for some women, it might just not turn them on, and that's up to them.

With that in mind, most bi men choose to remain silent. Why come out when it means fewer women will be interested in dating you? Let's also factor in the changing times of just how far we've come in a short space of time. Most of the married bi men reaching out to me are in their 40s or 50s. They grew up in a vastly more homophobic world than the one we live in now – and it's not as if the present is some LGBTQ+ utopia. There was no equal marriage when they joined the dating pool. For many previous generations of bi men, ending up with a man would be a far worse place to be. As a result, many bi men did their best to try to be with women. It's unhealthy: as a bisexual, forcing yourself to choose a gender is unnatural. Some would call it privilege, but I'd call it a curse. It feels as though we can choose to be safe, and maybe we can, but living an unfulfilled life where you can't be the authentic you doesn't sound very privileged to me.

A lot of men who found themselves in this situation followed the straight handbook, dated a woman, fell in love, got married, bought a house, had babies. They buried their same-sex attractions as deep down as they possibly could, doing their best to convince themselves that this is what they wanted.

Then, one day, they wake up next to their wife and wonder, 'Does she love me or the straight character I've been playing all these years?' They fear they'll die and their wife won't have ever known the real them – did they actually find unconditional love or was it on the condition of only finding women attractive? Would their wife knowing they were bisexual really matter after all these years?

The world has also changed. Being attracted to someone of the same sex isn't the sin it was in the 1980s. There can be feelings of jealousy. Why do these young gays get to run around being happy without a care in the world when you've put yourself through so much? After everything, don't you deserve to be accepted by, at the very least, the people around you?

The problem is that you have been lying. You've been playing a character. And even the most understanding wife and loving marriage is going to be rocked by a later-in-life coming out. To answer the question on this one, it's never too late to come out, but this one in particular is going to be tricky.

So, how do you do it?

First things first. You need to be clear why you want to come out to your wife. If it's because you want to explore your sexuality and potentially have some same-sex liaisons, that's a different situation that we'll explore later. This situation is specifically about wanting to tell your wife about your sexuality because you want to be honest and accepted for the real you.

I always think one of the best things you can do is

talk about other people in the same situation, so maybe bring up a celebrity, TV character or friend who came out in later life. Get your wife talking about what she thinks, stress how hard it must have been for the man involved. This helps you at least understand where her head is at with the concept, possibly even what her worries would be, and hopefully you can guide her to looking at the situation empathetically.

Sooner or later, though, you'll have to bite the bullet and tell her. I'd say it's best for you to take her on the journey with you, explain why you made the decisions you did and convey your fear that she might not have married you if she'd have known. Explain why you're coming clean now and what it means to you for her to know the truth.

Then get ready for a long evening of questions while she tries to make sense of it. From all I've learned over the years, the main theme of what she'll want to know is how this news will change her life. Usually, the answer is not much at all. (Unless this is the start of you wanting to open up the relationship to explore your bisexuality.)

Reassuring her that she is the one for you and this is about honesty rather than a change in your relationship should help the situation. No detail is too small. Will you now be commenting on when a hot man walks past? Will you want to be pegged? Is this just an FYI conversation and it's not to be mentioned again?

It's also important to remind her what she does know. She knows you. And, aware of your sexuality or not, she's been in a relationship with a bisexual man for a long time.

The only thing that's really changing is that now she knows about it.

The one thing you might have to give this situation is time. You can't expect her to know what she wants to ask and organize her emotions in one evening. Things may come to her over the coming days and months. Keep the conversation open and work towards a relationship that you're both happy with.

Is it too late to let my husband know I'm bisexual?

While a less common scenario, there are many bi women that find themselves in a similar situation to the one above. They feel that they have left it too late to come out to their husband and wonder whether the revelation will impact the dynamics of the relationship.

There is a perception that a wife coming out to a husband would be his dream: does this mean threesomes? And therein lies the first issue: that you will be over-sexualized. And there's the worry that your partner might use your coming out as a gateway to infidelity or opening up the relationship.

On the flip side, there is also the worry that your husband might feel that you aren't satisfied by him. That you want a sexual experience or a closeness that he simply can't provide. It can cause a lot of anxiety in men; they suddenly fear they aren't enough for you and start to let paranoia infect the relationship.

I also think that a lot of bi women are concerned that

they will come off as 'attention seeking' and that their partner might think they are making it up to create drama. The worry that your bisexuality could be dismissed and how that might impact on how you feel about your husband can be equally frightening.

The truth on this one is that the answer is much the same as above. Regardless of gender, having an open and honest conversation is the only way through, explaining to your husband why you've kept this secret, why you're choosing to open up now and what your fears are. It's again important to explain how you see this revelation changing your relationship. Do you want an open relationship? Is this just an FYI? Do you want to discuss women you find attractive?

You could also say that society's attitudes towards bisexuality have evolved over time, and it's possible that your husband's understanding of bisexuality may have changed or become more accepting since the beginning of your relationship. Perhaps part of the reason you are coming out now is that you feel he would be more accepting and see you for you rather than some fantasy. You should also stress the importance of trust and honesty in your relationship. Try explaining that you're sharing this information now because you want to be open and authentic with him.

Coming out later in a relationship is always tricky. Be patient; it's a process. But remember, he's always been married to a bi woman; it's just that now he knows.

Is it too late to come out to my same-sex spouse?

Many might assume that coming out to someone who is LGBTQ+ themselves would be less daunting, but believe me that's not always the case. There are many bi men and women that feel they can't be honest about their opposite-sex attractions, and with the entire world seeing them in a same-sex relationship, including their spouse, it's better to just appear gay/lesbian.

I've had many bi men over the years tell me that they are bi but it's too late for them; all their friends are gay, they have a boyfriend and they have only ever dated men – who would believe them? I've also had bi women tell me that they are afraid about coming out as bi to their partner because they worry that she would 'freak out' or feel betrayed. Some even worry their partner might leave if they view her as less than a 'pure lesbian'. These situations are both hard to manage, but many bi people are driven to want to come out, to be accepted by their other half for who they truly are, and can sometimes feel resentment at the idea they could be rejected by other LGBTQ+ people who preach tolerance.

If you are looking to come out to a same-sex spouse, in my experience, the bit you need to be prepared for is the disbelief. I've heard of a lot of bi people who have come out only to be treated with scepticism by their other half. They might, for example, say that you've never shown an interest in someone of the opposite sex and don't understand where it is coming from. You have to explain to them that even though they may not have personally seen it, it is how you've been feeling and these are your attractions.

Another aspect you might have to face is 'Why now?' Have you had enough of the relationship and want something different? Of course, I can't tell you why you're coming out now, but I can tell you that times are changing. Years ago, and still in some cases to this day, a bisexual may have just accepted the status quo. Sentenced to a life being seen as gay or lesbian and just getting on with it. Now, bisexuals are becoming more visible, and there is also a greater emphasis on other LGBTQ+ identities outside of being gay or lesbian. If you've gone through the trouble of coming out once, you might feel inauthentic still having to live under the wrong label, and why should you? Explaining this can help – that although it might be easier for them and the world around you to put a label they are comfortable with on you, it's not the correct one, so they and the world are just going to have to live with it.

Explain that this revelation is about your personal journey of self-discovery and authenticity. It's not a reflection of your dissatisfaction with the relationship. Assure your spouse that your love and commitment remain unchanged.

My hope for all of you is that coming out to your partner is a loving experience that bonds you even more tightly. But that is not always the case. In those moments, it can be helpful to reflect back the comments they make. Ask them if what they have said to you is what their father said to them when they came out. Ask them why the acceptance of the queer community doesn't extend to bisexuals. Stay firm and strong. As I say, you would imagine that coming out to someone who is queer would be easier, but I know that it can be anything but. Just know that you deserve acceptance and aren't asking for anything more than they ask for by being open and gay/lesbian.

Potential partners hate my bisexuality. Should I go back in the closet?

For some bisexuals, constant rejection can become too much to take. Sadly, bi people can experience this rejection from their own partners.

The idea that you would be better off back in the closet is not an uncommon thought. It's particularly hard when you are a few weeks or months into a relationship and realize that your bisexuality is a deal breaker.

My advice is really to persevere in this situation. As unbelievable as it may seem at the time, bisexuals do find partners. Eventually, you will find someone that accepts you for you. Have enough respect for yourself that you demand a partner that accepts you, not one who needs you to play a gay/straight role. There are so many happy bisexuals out there in validating relationships where their bisexuality isn't an issue. Please don't lose faith and hide yourself or accept a partner that isn't a good match. Keep going – they are out there.

Everyone thinks I'm straight. Will I lose my friends if I come out as bi?

One of the issues all people with same-sex attractions can experience is same-sex friends feeling your coming out changes the dynamic between you. When you're considering coming out, a big factor for a lot of people is how it will impact their friendships. So often we worry about rejection, but sensing a fundamental change in your relationship can be just as heartbreaking.

What's worse, it's not always a big moment or conversation; it can be tiny changes – such as your best friend no longer feeling comfortable getting changed in front of you or not inviting you to sleepovers.

With this situation, you have to be reasonable. For some people, the fact that you are attracted to their gender may change things. You don't have a right to see them naked or to sleep in their bed. Maybe there are some boundaries they might want to put in place. If possible, you should look at this as an evolution of your friendship. Things are changing, but as long as the bond is there and the friendship is still meaningful to you both, a few little changes should be manageable.

It goes without saying, but it's always helpful to let your friend know that while you find their gender attractive, you don't find them personally attractive. Maybe even give a few funny reasons why you don't find them attractive.

You can also look to include them in your journey. Discuss your same-sex attractions, tell them who you find hot, share funny fail stories from your attempts at gay sex. Including them in the journey will demystify it for them and make them realize that regardless of the gender you're dating, you're still you.

Ultimately, you don't need friends who are going to make you feel bad about who you are, and it is a matter of self-care and self-respect to not put up with that. If the friendship changes irreparably and being bi does prove too much for them to handle, it might be time to phase them out. As sad as it is, we all deserve to have friends who celebrate us. Life is too short to simply make do.

What is the best way to come out to my kids as bisexual?

Coming out to your children is something almost unique to bisexual people. For most same-sex couples, it will be pretty obvious to the children that they have two mommies or two daddies. But if to the outside world your relationship looks straight, a conversation may need to be had.

A big factor in how to approach this question is the age of your children.

If your kids are very young, then I would say it's more about raising them in a way that you don't hide it rather than a big coming-out conversation. For example, in our house there is a picture of me at Pride where I'm wearing a bisexual T-shirt. One day, when my kids can read, they might ask about it. Another example would be that as they get older, if I am ever nosey enough to ask if there are any kids at school they *like like*, I'll be sure to ask if there are any girls or boys. If they question this, it's a good segue into 'Well, daddy likes men and women'.

If your kids are older, then it might be that a conversation needs to be had, especially if you're in the process of a more wider coming out. As with most other coming-out scenarios, just explain how this will impact their lives. Will you be leaving their mother or father or is it an FYI? Take them on the journey with you; let them know why you're telling them now and why you kept it hidden. Don't forget to remind them that they've always had a bi parent – it's just that now they know about it.

Kids are amazing and they tend to surprise you in the best ways. My stepson was eight years old when he turned around and asked his mother if I was bisexual. It made the previous few weeks of me agonizing over the best way to tell him irrelevant. I also once received a letter from a bi father who was planning to come out to his children, only to have his son come out as bi to him. Interestingly, this made the father want to delay his own coming out so as not to steal his son's thunder.

Will my partner think my bisexuality makes me a cheating risk?

For many bisexuals, their ability to be attracted to more than one gender will go hand in hand with people suspecting they are more at risk of cheating. For some reason, people think we are attracted to everyone on the planet, with their logic concluding that it will all eventually be too much and we'll have to give in and cheat. Its rude, offensive and inaccurate.

If you're in a relationship with someone who seems to feel this way, it's time for a make-or-break conversation. Maybe go with the most obvious point: that cheating is a character trait, not a sexuality trait. To suggest a sexuality makes you more likely to cheat just makes them sound like they don't have a good grasp of the situation. Remind them how many gay and straight people cheat and have affairs. Your bisexuality isn't the problem, and they wouldn't be any more protected from a partner cheating if they were dating a straight person.

Ultimately, trust is trust, and if they don't have it for you, there is nothing you can do. You must stand your ground on this one. Don't dance to their tune or change your behaviour in order to prove you're trustworthy to them. No, you won't be home by a certain time; no, you won't uninvite yourself to a friend's sleepover; and you certainly won't let them check your phone (if they only now want to do that upon discovering you're bisexual). A lack of trust because of your sexuality is baseless; tell them you expect them to pull themselves together or else a conversation about the relationship working is needed.

Will coming out as bisexual ruin my social status?

For some bi people, reluctance to come out might not

actually be a worry about how those closest to you might react; for many, the worry can be about the wider community. These communities can take many forms. Those who are religious might be worried about how others in the faith might see them. Others may live in neighbourhoods where everyone knows everyone's business. Some might even consider their wider community to be their sports team or the PTA.

This issue has been observed in studies. One piece of research that looked at this issue in men found that males who have a household income of $30,000 or more per year reported greater concealment about their same-sex behaviour than men with lower incomes (Columbia University Mailman School of Public Health, 2013). While not conclusive, it supports the theory that the more social status you have, the greater the chance you'll wish to remain closeted.

For those worried about this, the honest truth is that, unfortunately, it probably will impact your social status. That's just the reality of more people being involved. When more people know about your bisexuality, a greater variety of reactions are possible. In the modern world, more and more famous people and people in positions of power appear to be coming out, with a mixed response across the board.

The only advice I could give here is that whether you're a Premier League footballer or a prominent member of your local church, you are in a lucky position by being well known. This brings with it some power, which gives you the opportunity to do good by coming out. Yes, it might be hard for you, yes, it might lose you some followers on Instagram, but, ultimately, if you don't take the risk, it's not going to be any easier for the next person. You have the opportunity to use your power and clout to change the world for bisexual people. To stand strong, to be visible and to be seen. I'm a big believer that if you have strength to spare as a bisexual, you must use it to help the bisexuals who are struggling and pave the way for a better bi tomorrow.

Ultimately, if you're worried about coming out publicly because of how it will impact your profile, it's a result of previous bisexuals being scared of the same thing and choosing to remain hidden. Will you continue the cycle? Or will you be one of the bisexuals who decide the buck stops with you and kick open those doors, bringing bi-visibility to all you meet?

RELATIONSHIPS

What does a bisexual relationship even look like?

One of the things we don't talk about enough is what does a successful relationship look like when one or more of the people in the relationship is bisexual? In contrast, we talk endlessly about the issues bisexuality poses in a relationship. One of the big stigmas is that a bisexual person in a relationship can never be truly satisfied because we need to have a healthy mix of genders to be happy.

We know this is nonsense, but it doesn't help that some bisexual people do seem to struggle balancing their bisexuality with a monogamous relationship. Many people have written to me about this over the years. Some are in opposite-sex relationships and feel unsure how to display their bisexuality or feel that their 'straight-facing' relationship means they no longer 'qualify' as being queer.

The unfortunate truth is that we don't have many

examples of what being in a relationship as a bisexual looks like. Although queer representation in TV and films has improved, the same can't often be said for bisexual representation. In entertainment, most of us will have seen a relationship between two gay men, but little representation of a gay man in a relationship with a bi man. Similarly for bi women: in the few examples we have, we often don't see a bi woman or two bi women depicted in a relationship together. I've often made the case that we've only ever seen same-sex love explored through gay eyes.

A same-sex relationship doesn't always entail two gay/lesbian partners; likewise, an opposite-sex relationship doesn't always have two straight partners. This lack of seeing ourselves played out in the media or even in real life in our close circles gives us fewer touchpoints to help us understand our own happiness in our relationships.

So, what's a bi to do?

It sounds corny and it will be different for everyone, but it really is about building a relationship that works for you. Some of this might come with experience. For example, I've known a lot of people early on in their bi journey who thought that free love and open relationships were what they wanted, only to make the horrific discovery that it wasn't by watching someone else having sex with their partner. Sometimes, you won't know until you try, and the truth is, you are going to fall over and make mistakes on the road to figuring out what relationship success looks like to you.

For most people, being in a relationship is also about

the other person being happy and fulfilled. That's no different for bisexual people. What is different is the role gender can play in relationships and how that impacts your position. For instance, if you're in a same-sex relationship, the dynamics tend to be more equal; jobs around the house are decided on skill sets rather than gender stereotypes. If you then find yourself in an opposite-sex relationship, the expectations can shift based on gender. If you're a man, it's possible you might be expected to take on a protector role, keeping your woman safe from all the dragons and goblins out there. And if you're a woman, you might be expected to take on a more maternal role, let the man lead or be the one that looks after the emotional well-being in the home. With these elements in mind, it can be trickier for bi people to be confident in the position they play in the relationship as it changes with each partner.

If you do find yourself in an opposite-sex relationship, you will have to decide how your queer side is displayed. This can be difficult for bisexuals, and I've received many questions on it over the years. While it might come as a surprise for some, going out waving flags and throwing glitter around the place doesn't come naturally to all of us. Some people are reserved and don't feel comfortable being 'out there' discussing their sexuality or holding banners. That's not to say they don't want to be seen as bisexual, and many can start to resent their situation because they feel that they've been forced back into the closet. There are, however, many ways around this, such as being out on social media or being part of an LGBTQ+ group.

The path to success in a relationship starts with talking – communication with your partner about your bisexuality, what it means to you and how you'd like to display it. You'll have to work on it – don't expect it to be perfect straight away – but you need to decide collectively what good looks like.

Success as a bisexual in a relationship is about being happy in the relationship; it's also about feeling that your bisexuality is celebrated not tolerated; that your partner gets it and is happy with the way you display it, and that you don't feel any topic is taboo to talk about.

I'm worried my partner knows I watch porn. How can I approach the subject?

Being worried about your porn use while in a relationship can be common for many people, regardless of their gender or sexuality. However, for bisexual people, the issue seems to be inflated, taboo and riddled with stigma.

When approaching this topic, the first thing we have to be firm on is that we aren't going to be held to standards that non-bisexual people aren't held to. Men and women, whether straight or gay, watch porn all the time; in many relationships, it's factored in as a given and completely normal. When bi men and women do the same, it's seen to mean something deeper.

Over the years, I've had many bi men 'admit' to me that they watch gay porn while in a relationship with a woman. As though it is something to be ashamed of. It isn't, but it does touch a nerve for us. As the stigma goes, 'bi people can't be happy with one gender; they won't be able to be satisfied in a relationship and will probably end up gay'. While we know this is nonsense, we can't escape that it's in the back of our minds, like the teacher at school who told you that you'd grow up to be a failure. For many bisexuals in opposite-sex relationships, watching gay porn can make them feel as though the biphobic prophecies are coming true, that maybe it's a sign they aren't satisfied; that if they are watching gay porn when they could be having sex with their girlfriend, then maybe they are gay, after all. It's self-doubt, pure and simple.

All I can do is tell you that this is not the case and ask you once again to consider why straight men who watch porn in relationships aren't painted with the same brush. No one is suggesting that because a straight man is watching porn that features a threesome, he couldn't possibly be fulfilled in a relationship with just his girlfriend. As bisexuals, sometimes we can overthink things, and I find that we tend to be much too hard on ourselves.

Because I know that so many bisexuals struggle with this issue, it's only natural that the partners of bisexuals may also struggle. Our partners are often the targets of stigma themselves, with many people only too happy to ask, 'Aren't you worried they'll cheat on you?' or the standard, 'What if they leave you for a man?' While many people won't be bound by the stigma, it can niggle in there sometimes, and finding out that your bi partner is watching same-sex porn can be challenging for some people.

If you are in this situation, explaining it as I have above might just do the trick. Would they worry about porn use if you were a straight man/woman? Let's not ignore the fact that the answer might be yes. Some people do see it as an insult to know that their partner watches porn or even masturbates. If this is the issue, that's where you can put this book down for a while and start scrolling through Google, because that isn't a bi-specific issue. You're in good company, and I'm sure there are lots of sites out there offering advice on porn use in relationships.

The only thing I would say about porn and masturbation, personally, is *be careful*. I'm not anti-porn or anti-masturbation, but we have to realize, as bisexuals, that we can become over-dependent on the stuff. Porn site Xhamster revealed a few years ago that users who visit adult sites several times a day are more than twice as likely to identify as bisexual as those who visit only once a week (Kaplan, 2022).

For many bisexuals I know, porn can be an amazing outlet, allowing us to live out our bisexual fantasies (not to be confused with actions we would necessarily want to take in real life). We just don't want to become dependent.

I always think that we only have so much sexual energy – why waste it watching other people have sex? Have your own sexual adventures (with consenting partners). Yes, sometimes your partner might not be in the mood or there might be a sexual fantasy they can't fulfil. In those moments, don't always turn to porn as the only way to get off. Close your eyes and create the fantasy yourself. We live in such a digital world, but wouldn't you rather cum to a sex fantasy you've made in your own mind rather than one thought up by some porn director?

As I say, this isn't an anti-porn rant, but I find that, for bisexuals, it's more important that we don't have our fantasies led by porn sites and the suggested next tab. We need to stay attuned to our bodies and hormones and really understand what we want sexually, and how that differs day to day.

As a final point on this one, your partner is unlikely to be overly concerned about your porn use if the two of you are having amazing sex yourselves. If you have gotten to a point where you'd rather watch porn than have sex with your partner, there is a problem, and in that situation, I'd tell you to go three months without porn or wanking, and see how you feel.

Whether porn-loving or not, it's important that you and your partner communicate and build a relationship that works for the both of you. Talking is always a good start. Maybe you see a request for you to stop watching porn as completely reasonable and something you're happy to do. Maybe it's a deal breaker and an important part of your sexual expression. Just don't let your bisexuality play a factor in how serious the issue is. Part of accepting you as bisexual is that they…accept you as bisexual. You have an attraction to people of the same gender – it's part of the gig.

My partner doesn't believe I'm bisexual. What should I do?

As much as I'd like to say that the answer to this question is a simple two-word answer – 'leave them' – I know that, in real life, it's a little harder than that.

What's more, it would make me a hypocrite; I've certainly dated people in the past who weren't 100 per cent comfortable with my bisexuality. It's easy to ignore it when you're constantly having amazing sex, drowning in chemistry and having an all-round good time. The truth is, a lot of people don't get it when it comes to bisexuality; add those to the people who outright would never date a bi person, and we'd be left with slim pickings if we didn't at least give it a go when someone seems to be struggling with accepting bisexuality.

In my experience, this has been more common in same-sex relationships, where bisexuality can sometimes be seen as a transitional phrase and not respected in its own right. Typically, it's not a deal breaker for them; they'll still have sex with us, date us, but they won't fully believe that we are bisexual. It can be as simple as rolling their eyes when we talk about our bisexuality or just never being willing to talk about it with us. I have met quite a few gay and lesbian people who have struggled to see sexuality outside of their own experience. Being attracted to the same gender made them identify as gay, so they wonder why that would be any different for bi people. Sometimes there can also be feelings of resentment: that they think you get to play both sides. Where possible, try to be empathetic – it can be a defence mechanism: they might worry they aren't enough for us and so hope we aren't *really* bi.

If you find yourself in the unfortunate situation where you feel a partner doesn't accept or believe in bisexuality, but something is telling you not to walk away, the best thing you can do is talk. Try to get to the bottom of what exactly the failure in their understanding is. Be realistic with your expectations; don't feel that you're going to have the answers immediately. Hear them out, go away and think about it, then raise the issue again and give your responses. The good thing about bi-ignorance is that it rarely evolves or grows. It's pretty basic, and once you've developed some strong responses to their comments, they usually have little room to keep going with their argument.

Eventually, you'll reach a point with them where you'll know if this is something they do accept or could accept eventually. You may also get to the point where you realize that it's not in their nature or capacity to understand, to truly get bisexuality and accept you for it. It's then on you to decide if you can live with it or if you'd rather be in a relationship where you aren't just tolerated but celebrated for who you are.

Don't let self-doubt or fear influence your decision. There are many people out there who would celebrate their bisexual partner. So, the argument that the world is full of biphobes who would never accept you anyway, and that it's better the devil you know, doesn't hold water.

Eventually, it comes down to how important your bi-sexuality is to you. As an author of a book on bisexuality, I clearly think it's pretty damn important, and I wouldn't be able to have a long-term relationship with someone who had an issue with it. That said, I know for some people, their bisexuality just isn't that big of a deal to them, and that's fine.

Relationships are about compromise and accepting the other person, and if you're accepting of your partner's differences but they can't accept your sexuality, I'd say that's pretty telling.

Is my bisexuality changing?

One of the things no bisexual is immune to is that their attractions can appear to shift over time. This is totally normal, but there aren't many people around to tell you that. Changes also differ from bisexual to bisexual. Some can tend to feel more attracted to one gender in particular every few weeks; for others, it can be a few years. There is also the factor of being in a relationship – some bisexuals feel that they no longer notice people outside of their part-ner and wonder if they have actually become gay/straight. Others worry that they can't stop noticing a gender dif-ferent to the one of their partner, perhaps watching lots of same-sex porn when in an opposite-sex relationship, which leads them to wonder if they are now gay or at least more attracted to the same sex than they were.

It's all totally normal, but as bisexuals in the modern

world, we tend to overthink the changes. Let's not forget, many in the world around us tell us that our bisexuality is some sort of phase we are working through, so when you do notice changes in your attractions, it's easy to assume the worst.

The real trick is knowing what, if anything, you should do about it. My advice is to lean into your attractions. If this week you're being drawn to how attractive men are, enjoy how attractive men are. If you feel like this month you've gone off women, no one is forcing you to look at them. Accept and embrace that your attractions are fluid to a degree and certain things might be on your mind or catching your eye more at some points than others.

It's just like anything else: sometimes we go through a phase of wanting to listen to certain music or watch certain films. Sometimes we want to go clubbing more than we do at other times. We don't tend to overthink those things, so why should we overthink this? It is, however, important to recognize that you are still you and that you are still bisexual. You aren't swinging from gay to straight to bi. You're bisexual and you have the potential to be attracted to more than one gender. Feeling like your attractions are shifting or certain things are more attractive at different points is part of the gig.

Of course, this is a lot easier said than done if you're in a relationship. If a partner feels you're no longer as attracted to them as you were before, then that is a factor that needs addressing. This is where self-understanding and communication is key. You need to make sure your partner doesn't feel rejected, while at the same time not forcing yourself to do things that don't feel natural at the moment. In these instances, it's important to take a step back and consider that straight people also experience these issues. Sometimes straight people go off sex. Sometimes straight people can't stop thinking about the hot girl/guy/person at the office. It doesn't always spell the end of their relationship – but it can spell problems if they don't communicate and discuss their issues in a way that works for them.

As I say, the first step in this is understanding yourself. First, you might be the kind of bisexual who cannot ignore your sexual urges for different genders, to the point you want to be regularly acting on those feelings. If this is the case, you're going to need some form of open relationship. Second, you might not identify as bisexual but sometimes you desire same-sex relations, and when you act on these desires, you view it as 'getting it out of your system'. As these desires are infrequent, you might not want to make a big deal of it, but the above perspective might be a coping mechanism – a way to avoid engaging with your sexuality. Understanding yourself must lead to transparency about your sexuality and being honest about who and what genders you desire.

For others, it's not so much that they want to have sex with someone; it's actually that they don't feel like having sex with their partner. If that is the case, having a conversation is going to be of the utmost importance. I go back to the straight people example – sometimes they go through a period of not wanting sex, and that's okay. If you feel this way, think outside the box. Maybe you've just gone off penetrative sex – what better excuse to mix it up and find other ways to be intimate?

I think the most worrying scenario can be when you're not used to experiencing changes in your attraction levels and then a sustained period comes along. At these times, the most comforting thing I can say is that these periods do pass eventually. It's no reason to overthink or to rearrange your life.

All people of all sexualities have a fluid experience. Sometimes blowjobs seem amazing – then for a couple of months, they don't. Sometimes women with long blonde hair are all you can think about – and then, suddenly, along walks a brunette. Give yourself a break, work with the natural drumbeats of your sexuality and do your best to enjoy the experience.

Coming out as bi has cost me my gay friends. Is there a way to get them back?

It's not uncommon for a bisexual to be kicked out of their gay pack (or at least be made to feel unwelcome) when their bisexuality becomes something that can no longer be ignored.

I experienced this myself, and it's absolutely infuriating. At the time, I'd just broken up with my boyfriend of two and a half years. This meant that, despite me telling my friends that I was bi, they'd spent years seeing me in a 'gay' relationship, which they were comfortable with – it made me like them.

Once that relationship ended, and I was all of a sudden dating again and kissing all the girls and boys, their uncomfortableness became apparent. I recall one evening in particular when we left a bar, and I ended up kissing a girl I'd met inside. Much to my surprise, the next day an image of said kiss appeared on a group chat between myself and a group of my gay friends. Not only had one of my gay friends taken this picture to embarrass me, but the caption read something along the lines of 'Disgusting, a gay man kissing a girl outside a gay bar'. The replies to the message weren't easy reading either.

The messages told me all I needed to know. Now that I wasn't with a man and had dared to act on my bisexuality, the friendship was over. At best, they could maybe keep me around as a specimen to laugh at and examine, like some pet that's a conversation starter. But they'd never see me as one of them, or the same again.

The truth is many gay and lesbian friendships are founded on the principle that they share a sexuality and all that comes with it. It's about strength in numbers, learning from each other, sharing experiences.

The unfortunate reality is many bi people don't find a loving LGBTQ+ community. In fact, in 2018, Stonewall found that 27 per cent of bi women and 18 per cent of bi men have experienced biphobia from within the LGBTQ+ community (Glass, 2018). Similarly, a report by the Equality Network found that 66 per cent of bisexuals only felt 'a little' or 'not at all' part of the LGBTQ+ community (Rankin, Morton and Bell, 2015).

Of course, there are many wonderful accepting gay and lesbian people out there, so really the question becomes whether you want to keep biphobic/bi-ignorant friends when there are so many amazing people in the world you could spend your time with.

You should try speaking with your friends and make them see you are still the same person, but the reality is that coming out can cost you relationships. Many assume it's the relationships with straight people that can suffer by coming out, but for bi people, our relationships with our gay friends can just as easily disintegrate. This is simply something we have to accept.

Ultimately, put yourself first. If you do want to fight for your friendships, then give it a go. You must, however, be ready to end toxic friendships once you realize there is no going back to the way things were.

How do I approach the subject of an open relationship?

Some bi people do find that the best relationship that works for them is an open one. This allows them to have sexual relationships with multiple partners while still maintaining both a sexual and romantic relationship with their primary partner.

If you are in a relationship and decide this is something

you want to explore, then approaching your partner has to be handled the right way.

The first factor you need to consider is whether you do really want an open relationship. In my experience, a lot of people say that they do, but so few of them can make it work. I've seen it go wrong. Very wrong. Do be cautious. That said, I've also heard of many people who do make it work, so it is possible.

Over the years, I've had many bi people reach out to me on this topic. Their stories are usually similar. They knew they were bi but decided to hide it. Now they are married but feel that they missed out on never acting upon their same-sex attractions. They now want to know if an open relationship could be the answer to them finally getting to have that experience.

The first thing I usually tell bi people in this situation is that sex isn't that great. If you've spent a lot of time imagining what sex with the same gender would be like – watching porn, perhaps – it's not going to be as hot as you think. It will probably be over very quickly and won't live up to the fantasy. I like to say that to really manage people's expectations of what this experience will be like. In life in general, we spend a lot of time thinking about what we don't have and not enough appreciating what we do have.

So, once you've considered whether it is something you really want to do, and you have realistic expectations of what it will be like, the final step is to consider the risk. An open relationship, and even the suggestion of it, could end your relationship. Some people will be instantly horrified that you want to have sex with other people, and it could change the way they view the relationship going forward. Others might be willing to give it a try but, once they know you've had sex with another person, realize how deeply uncomfortable and betrayed they feel.

If you've added up the pros and cons and are still convinced an open relationship is the way to go, approaching your partner must be done the right way.

I'd suggest first asking the question under the radar. Find a way to ask them, 'What do you think of open relationships?' It might be helpful to have watched a film that features a successful one so the question seems natural. Asking them what they think of the concept first, rather than asking straight out for an open relationship, allows them to be more honest. It also means you can get a clear understanding of their positive and negative feelings on the topic.

Depending on how it goes, I'd suggest raising the issue a few more times over the next few weeks, each time tackling any concerns that they have and painting a positive picture of an open relationship. This will also allow them to understand it's on your mind.

Eventually, you can work up to asking them if they would be willing to try an open relationship together. I'd be prepared to paint a picture of exactly how you see an open relationship working. Of course, this should be a collaboration, but at least have suggestions so that they know you are taking it seriously.

Think of it as suggesting going on holiday. You wouldn't just say, 'Let's go on holiday.' You'd say where and why you'd picked it, what the dates would be.

So, how would this open relationship work? What would the rules be? Is there a time limit, a date to review how it's going? How will you find people? How many times can you sleep with the same person? What if their mum finds out? How do they know you won't leave them if you have amazing sex with someone else? You need to have answers for all their concerns.

Is it too soon to settle down?

As bisexuals, sometimes it's really hard to know when it's the right time to settle down. I know some bisexuals who say they 'aren't done yet'. This can be for many reasons. Some are working through a sexual checklist; maybe they haven't done the orgy yet or they haven't had the circle jerk experience. Others are simply having too much fun, and the thrill of meeting new people for a date with the chance of sex later might be too much of a good time to give up.

These can also be balanced with a ticking clock. I've known many women worried about how many eggs they have left, and the pressure to find the right partner has become all-consuming and stressful. Equally, you might be thinking about how your parents had a five-year-old by the time they were your age. Perhaps most of your friends are getting married and you're still waking up next to a different person each Saturday.

Some bisexuals may have never explored their bisexuality. Maybe they've only ever dated men. Now Prince Charming has shown up and suddenly you're confronted with the idea that you may never get to have an experience with a woman. Is it worth rejecting Prince Charming until you have explored your bisexuality so that you can make sure you're *really ready* to settle down?

It can feel as though bisexuality adds an extra layer of doubt to knowing if it is the right time to settle down. But the truth is, we aren't that unique; people of all sexualities have doubts about when it is the right time to commit. There are many straight guys out there who might feel like they haven't slept with enough women to settle down. Or women who might feel as though they haven't met the right person yet. So, the first thing to do is not blame your bisexuality. Not knowing is normal, whatever your sexuality.

So, how is a bi to know when it's the right time? Ultimately, it's not about you deciding when the time is right; it's actually about the right person coming along. If you have an open heart and are receptive to the potential of love, when that right person comes along, you'll know.

I experienced this first-hand when I met my (now) fiancée and mother of my children. Settling down couldn't have been further from my mind when we met. I had only been single for six months, and I was having the time of my life. I was swinging from men to women, sleeping with everyone and being my best bisexual self. I had finally come into my bisexuality, accepted who I was and was actually getting to live my truth. I didn't want to be in a relationship; I had orgies to attend, men to sleep with, women to pleasure. But there she was. After meeting her, I actually remember thinking to myself, 'For fuck's sake'. I knew she was the one – trust her to show up when I wasn't looking for her. But there wasn't really a hesitation in my mind. Could I have gone on for another few years having sex with random people and seeking out new and different sexual experiences? Sure. But none of that was worth passing up being with 'the one'. To be honest, the thought of all the experiences I'd be losing faded quite quickly as we embarked on our relationship. I was enjoying myself with her, I was happy – and I still am today.

I guess the moral of my story is that you can have all the theories you like about when is the right time to settle down, but when you find the right person, it's all going out the window. Suddenly, the things you're worried about losing will be eclipsed by what you're gaining. No, it doesn't mean your hormones and sexual fantasies are going to turn off. You'll still have urges – some of which might never be satisfied by your partner – but it's a small price to pay. I'd rather have what I have now than some cheap orgasm with a stranger that is over too quickly anyway.

Of course, my monogamous relationship isn't for everyone. Maybe you'll find someone who is open to an open relationship, and if that's something you want too, then maybe this issue won't be such a big one for you. But taking sex out of it for a moment, even if you have an open relationship, finding someone to partner with emotionally is still a big deal. When the world tells you that you have more options than most, getting it wrong can feel like it's your fault. What if this person can't support you emotionally? What if they are selfish? What if you end up living a life you never wanted, just to make them happy?

Ultimately, being bisexual doesn't give you superpowers to see into the future. Sometimes you have to take a leap of faith. Listen to your gut, check in with your hormones, and if you find them annoyingly cute or hot, go for it. If it all goes wrong, it goes wrong – how were you to know?

Whatever your position and feelings on this, it's important not to put your issues on to your partner. You don't want them to feel as though you have sacrificed part of who you are just to make them happy or that they are some sort of consolation prize. Let's not forget, for some bisexuals reading this, the reality will be that you actually aren't ready to settle down. That you just aren't ready to commit because there are parts of single life you haven't finished exploring. If you know this to be true, there is no point lying to yourself or a potential partner. The best thing to do is be honest and hope that in a few years your paths cross again and this time you'll both be in a receptive place.

I want kids. Should I be with
someone of the opposite sex?

Bisexuals are in a very unique situation compared with our gay and lesbian counterparts, particularly when it comes to children. Both cisgender gay and lesbian people know even before they meet their partner that having biological kids with them is a scientific impossibility (for now). For bisexuals, our ability to have biological children is determined by the sex of our partner. Should we meet a partner with an opposite set of genitalia to ours, then, boom, we're in the baby-making business. If not, the path to parenthood is going to be trickier.

This reality can weigh heavily on bisexuals who know that they want to be parents someday, and it can really mess with everything. Some bisexuals might set out to settle down eventually with someone of the opposite gender for this reason alone. As someone who's met a lot of bisexuals, I have concluded that this plan is flawed. If you're bi and open to dating more than one gender, there is just no way to ensure the sex of the person you're going to end up with. Say you're a bi guy who meets a really nice gay guy. You spend years together in a loving relationship – there's no way you're going to end it to go and be single again in search of a woman just because she has a working womb. You're more likely to want to work with your partner to find a solution to your missing-womb problem and explore options like surrogacy or adoption.

If we remove this idea of a game plan, you're back to a

50/50 chance of ending up with someone with the womb or sperm you need. If you do end up with someone with matching genitalia, it's important not to make them feel guilty. They will be more than aware that if you'd played your cards differently, biological children wouldn't be a hurdle for you. It's also important for you to let go of that thought internally. Resenting your partner isn't healthy; you have to trust that you're in this together, that you chose them for a reason and that this is just part of your journey. When you find the answer, it will be the right thing for you. It can also help to remember that even if you found someone of the opposite sex, you could still have fertility issues, or they could just straight up not want kids. With that in mind, if having children is important to you, then regardless of sex, it's important to bring that aspiration up early on in the relationship to ensure you're both on the same page and to avoid any nasty surprises further down the line.

Kids are a blessing, and speaking as a dad of three, writing this at 11.30 p.m. sitting next to my two-year-old daughter who has refused to go to sleep tonight, they're also an incredible amount of work. You'll be sleep deprived, you'll have to miss out on things you really wanted to do, you'll never stop worrying about them and they cost a bloody fortune. It's much better to go through all that with a loving partner who you chose because they were the right person for you than with one you chose because of their genitals.

How do I reassure my partner that they are enough for me?

For bisexuals in particular, there is a stigma that no one would be enough for us, due to our ability to find both men and women attractive. This belief is why some people flat out refuse to date us. Others, while they are open to dating us, worry that their bisexual partner might not be completely fulfilled by them.

As bi people and decent human beings, if your partner does feel this way, then we should try to help them see that we are fulfilled in the relationship.

Usually, the worry is around you being sexually satisfied – the idea that because they only have one set of genitalia, there are fantasies they can't fulfil.

There are a couple of routes you can take when approaching this topic. One is to consistently tell them how much the sex the two of you have is fulfilling. Let them know how lucky you are to have them and to have such amazing sex. I've also found humour to be great in this situation. Explain to them that you simply don't have the energy to have both a girlfriend and a boyfriend, that they're too much of a handful.

On the serious side, they do need to understand that just because you have the ability to be attracted to multiple genders, it doesn't mean that you need multiple genders to be happy. Try to explain it in terms that they understand. If they are worried that you'll miss giving a blowjob to another man, find something in their sexual history to compare it with. Maybe they dated a guy with more muscles than you or was taller than you. Maybe their last girlfriend had bigger boobs or long hair. How can you know they won't miss that?

It's also worth trying to find out what makes them jealous or what specifically they are worried about. This will help you avoid or at least manage their feelings. For example, maybe you act particularly flirty around same-sex friends. If that's not essential behaviour for you, maybe you could avoid doing it in front of your partner.

Time can really be a great healer with this issue. The consistency of a partner being reassured, feeling valued by you in a relationship and you being transparent with your sexuality and urges can make them feel that they are informed and secure.

What if my partner isn't enough after all?

One of the things both bi men and bi women have shared with me over the years is the fear that their partner isn't enough; that maybe they do want to go and have sex with someone whose gender is different to that of their partner. Perhaps they feel that, at this moment in time, they need female attention. Or they crave feeling the weight of a man on top of them.

This is hugely taboo. I mean, this is one of the main areas of prejudice aimed at bisexuals: that no one would ever be enough for us. Are the haters right? This fear of validating biphobic points of view can encourage bisexuals to bury these feelings deep inside, which is an equally unhelpful exercise.

Many of the men and women who reach out to me because they feel this way often didn't get a chance to explore their bisexuality. The stories are eerily similar: they knew they were bisexual but did their best to hide it. Eventually, they ended up in an opposite-sex relationship and now, years later, the fear they felt at the time about exploring their sexuality feels silly. They regret that they didn't explore it. They worry that they'll die without ever having an experience that feels natural to them.

Unexplored bisexuality is a terrible reality caused by biphobia. To have convinced a bi person their feelings are so wrong that they avoid them. To then have that bi person find themselves in a relationship and realize they now never will have those experiences is a very cruel truth.

Unpacking this issue, living with this issue and deciding what, if anything, to do about it is incredibly tricky, and differs from person to person.

Let's start with the positives. Someone experiencing worry that their partner isn't enough or that they didn't get to explore their bisexuality only feels that way because they are in a committed relationship. That's a fabulous place to be. Half the movies and songs that are put out are about people on their quest for love. Billions of pounds a year are spent on the search for love, but you already have it. Count that blessing. While your relationship might not be perfect, you have the power to improve it.

Second, I know I say this a lot, but bisexuals tend to overthink the situation. Having attractions outside of your partner is normal. Fantasizing about having sex with other people and feeling a connection with other people, those are normal – it doesn't mean that your partner isn't enough or that you can't fully commit to one person.

It is also normal in a relationship for things to get stale. You tend not to have as much sex as in the early days. Sometimes people start to wonder if they're missing out, not because of attractions from people outside of the relationship but from a feeling of not being fulfilled completely within it. If you are feeling that your partner isn't enough, don't let bisexuality be the scapegoat. Do an honest assessment of your relationship. Are you having enough sex? Are you being celebrated? Does caring for another person give you purpose? If there are issues, work on those and see if that changes things.

Some bisexuals who feel this way might consider cheating. Maybe a quick encounter with a stranger will scratch the itch and then you can get back to fully loving your partner? The truth is that such logic rarely works out for the best. It's also not worth risking your partner for a quick orgasm that will be over before you know it. Your relationship is worth far more than an evening with a sexy stranger.

However, for some bi people, trying monogamy can make them realize that it simply isn't for them. If that's the case, it's time to be honest with your partner and chat through your feelings. Hopefully, together you can find a solution that works for both parties.

Is it worth staying with my partner just to avoid the uncertainty of being bisexual and single?

Let me kick this one off by just saying the thing you aren't supposed to say: breaking up is harder for bisexual people than it is for gay and straight people.

There, I've said it. Don't bother tweeting your outrage at me; I don't read them. However, I will defend my position.

People who aren't bisexual tend to look at us and think we have so much choice – in fact, so much choice that they've labelled us greedy to make themselves feel better. However, there are consequences to having more options when it comes to the dating pool.

The truth is that the gender of your partner has a massive impact on your life. For example, it determines if you and your partner could naturally conceive a biological child. In some parts of the world, it determines if you can get married and even guarantees the safety of you and your partner in many places. More widely, it really can impact the 'culture' you experience day to day. As someone who has been in a long-term relationship with both a man and a woman, I do think that those day-to-day experiences, the people you are surrounded by and the topics of conversation differ greatly.

Straight and gay people are lucky in that sense. When they break up, their next partner will bind them to the same life experiences (obviously, there are variations, but you know what they are, and I won't bore you with them here). A gay man knows he's never going to be able to conceive naturally with his partner and can plan accordingly as well as accept the parameters of his relationship.

You can also factor in the social elements of how others view you. For example, if you're a man who's been in a relationship with a woman for five years and then moves on to dating a man, there are huge social changes. People will mistake you for being gay, and you might have to deal with random bursts of homophobia. Family members who said they accepted your bisexuality might now be singing a different tune when they actually see it in action.

Sex could also be different. Yes, we have attractions to more than one gender, but if you've become comfortable being the man in an opposite-sex relationship, the idea of having another man penetrate you can be daunting and confusing. Equally for women, perhaps going from a same-sex relationship to now having someone wanting to penetrate you or someone asking you to put on a strap-on does change that sexual dynamic.

It can also be uniquely unsettling. As I've mentioned, gay and straight people know the parameters they exist in. They know, regardless of who their partner is, their standing in the world would remain unchanged. Bisexuals don't have that. When they do get into a long-term relationship, that is the only moment they can really plan what a future would look like on the partner front, deciding if they want to adopt, how they might handle homophobia and so on. A breakup means going entirely back to the drawing board. They won't necessarily be able to plan for a natural conception. They won't know if their gay friends will be there for them if they suddenly go from dating a man to a woman. It's anxiety monosexual people can't truly empathize with.

For a bisexual, changing your partner means completely changing your way of life. It's for these reasons I say that breakups are harder for bisexual people.

What's more, far from the stigma that bisexuals are greedy tricksters who can't be committed, I actually believe the opposite is true. I think that as bisexuals we have a tendency to stick out a relationship even when it's clear it has become toxic.

One report found that sexual violence is more common against bisexual women than straight women or lesbians. Between 2015 and 2017, ONS figures show 11 per cent of bi women reported abuse by their partner, compared with 8 per cent of lesbians and 6 per cent of straight women (Glass, 2018).

Research suggests that bi people face unusually high rates of domestic violence. Sixty-one per cent of bisexual women have experienced rape, physical violence and/or stalking by an intimate partner in their lifetime, according to a CDC report, compared to 35 per cent of straight women and 44 per cent of lesbians. The statistics for bisexual men are similarly shocking with 37 per cent of bisexual men having faced violent acts in relationships, while 29 per cent of straight men and 26 per cent of gay men said the same (Centers for Disease Control and Prevention, 2010).

Getting back to the question at hand, the truth is that

only you will know if your relationship is worth fighting for. What I'm saying is that, as a bisexual, you need to be aware of the unique anxiety you can experience in this situation.

If the only reason you are choosing to stay in a relationship is because of the uncertainty being a single bi person brings, or at least if that's a big factor, my advice is to get out now.

Being scared is no reason to stay. It's not good for you and it's not good for them. Yes, it's scary, but this is the reality of bisexuality; this is your path. You'll have to be scared but do it anyway. Try to find the joy in being single and meeting new people rather than focusing on the worry of what you might be losing. Let's not forget, there's a chance you might end up with someone who is the same gender as your previous partner, and if you don't, by the time you realize, you'll already be head over heels for your new partner and it won't matter to you anyway.

My mum wants me to end up with someone of the opposite sex so that she can have grandkids. What should I tell her?

When it comes to bisexuality and family, some bizarre things can be said. Even if it's from a loving place, it can still be infuriating how little they understand about how bisexuality works.

When it comes to parents, it's not uncommon for them to be focused on how they're going to acquire grandchildren. People love a continuation of the bloodline. I've known many bisexuals who have been asked by a parent why they can't get with someone of the opposite gender to allow for the birth of children.

While their logic is correct – that biological children are a possibility – their understanding that we could choose to do that is misinformed at best.

If you are facing this, it's useful to explain that we can't go into sexuality with a game plan. We can't decide the gender of the person we are going to end up with any more than we could decide they are going to have blonde hair.

Love and human connection are tricky. If you're putting yourself out there to meet someone you want to spend the rest of your life with, you really don't know who you're going to click with, who is going to excite you, who you're going to fall in love with.

I think some parents genuinely believe that we can have fun while we are young and then do the right thing and settle down with someone to have children by a certain age. As if one day a calendar reminder is going to go off on your phone and you're going to turn to your same-sex partner and say, 'You know, even though this relationship is perfect, we have to break up because I promised my parents I'd find a nice woman/man to marry and have children with by the time I'm 32.' That's just not how real life works.

You can do your best to explain this to them. Some-times it's easier to put it in terms they would understand, such as, how would your mum feel if her parents had asked her to marry a doctor? Would she have rejected your dad because he didn't fit what her parents wanted? Or did her parents give her enough respect to go out there and find the person she felt was right for her?

My ex-boyfriend has asked me to wait a while before going public with my new girlfriend – out of respect for his pride. Is this unreasonable?

(This question could apply equally to a bi woman and her new boyfriend.)

Exes can be tricky to manage for bisexual people. In some instances, seeing you move on with a partner of a different gender can 'confirm' their suspicions – or those of their friends.

If you've gone from a woman to a man, or a man to a woman, depending on your gender, they might feel that you were really gay/straight all along. They may feel embarrassed because some biphobic people in their lives always told them you'd leave them for a man/woman eventually, or simply that you've wasted their time. Perhaps you have children together and they are worried about what the other parents at school may think when you come to pick up holding a man's hand. Will the children be bullied as a result?

Equally, if your previous partner was gay/lesbian, there could be resentment – the idea that they weren't 'gay enough' to keep you interested in a same-sex relationship.

There may be a genuine disbelief of the fact you could enjoy sex that doesn't require your partner to have a penis/vagina. Were you faking how much you enjoyed giving blowjobs? There could even be tinges of jealousy that you get to go and live a 'normal life' now. Was it always the game plan to end up with someone of the opposite sex? Were you just using them for fun in your 20s?

Depending on the terms on which your relationship ended, you may genuinely care about their feelings and not want anything to make them feel embarrassed or uncomfortable. If your former partner has asked for more time before they are forced to publicly explain your new relationship to their nearest and dearest, it's really on you to do what you're comfortable with.

I would, however, recommend involving your new partner. Getting their opinion can help to make them feel as if they are part of the process and not worry that you're still following the orders of your ex.

I also think it is important for you to put a time limit on such a request, if you do agree to it. Whether that be a month or six weeks, tell them firmly when they can expect that you'll be going public with your new partner.

On the other hand, if you do decide you don't want to be shackled by the demands of your ex, that is also okay, and you shouldn't feel any guilt. Your relationship is over, and you need to prioritize your current one. They may not like it at the time, but it will force them forward and they'll get over it eventually.

Am I cheating?

When you date a mixture of genders as well as people of different sexual orientations, some rules can be blurred. Bisexuals by nature tend to be more mature when it comes to understanding sex and relationships. Not to be rude, but a lot of straight and gay people can be very particular about the rules of a relationship. For instance, many straight people may feel it's completely inappropriate for a man and woman who are in relationships with other people to share a bed together. No ifs, no buts, it's just wrong. Despite the fact they aren't attracted to each other and don't plan to do anything sexual.

On the other hand, gay men who only really have gay friends might not see the issue with two gay guys who don't find each other attractive sharing a bed. Gay men also tend to be more willing to have open relationships, not caring that their other half likes to fuck other people, because they are confident that their relationship is the primary one. A recent Australian study found that gay couples' agreements regarding casual sex outside their relationships have changed markedly in the era of pre-exposure prophylaxis (PrEP). Nearly 40 per cent of PrEP users in relationships had agreements that allowed for condomless sex with casual partners (Samuel, 2019). Bisexuals exist in the chaotic place between these two realities. What might be appropriate in one culture could be totally taboo in the other.

What's more, if your gay boyfriend is allowed to stay in

the room while his best friend (who happens to be female) is getting changed, are you allowed to stay in the room while your best friend does the same? You could argue that the gay man doesn't find the female form appealing or sexual so it's fine for them to be alone while one of them is naked. So, should the bisexual leave the room while his friend is getting changed because he has the potential to find her body attractive? Side note: in both these scenarios, it would mean that the friend doesn't mind either way if you're in the room while they are getting changed. The point is that bisexuals are basically expected to follow both the straight *and* gay rule book on what is appropriate behaviour.

This can be isolating for bisexual people in relationships – basically, they don't trust us with anyone. If a straight man needs to be careful not to get too close to other women when he's in a relationship, then, by that logic, a bisexual in a relationship should be careful not to get too close to anyone. These differing logics on where the line is and what constitutes cheating set bisexual people up to fail.

That's why I would say it is imperative that once you agree to enter into an exclusive relationship with anyone, you have a conversation at your earliest convenience about what each of you considers cheating. The rules need to be set upfront rather than retrospectively deciding that you kissing a friend for a dare at a party was cheating.

You also need to think about ways your sexuality manifests and what you are comfortable giving up. For example, as a bi man dating a woman, you might agree that having sex with men is cheating, but what about watching gay porn? Perhaps you're part of a naked men's yoga group – is that still okay? If you're a bi woman, are you allowed to see other women naked? Is a sleepover at a female friend's house still allowed? Finding the line is important.

Remember, it's a negotiation; you don't have to agree to all their terms. For example, as part of the bisexual work I do, I've done a few photoshoots, some with implied nudity. This means that you have to be naked at the shoot and in front of the photographer. It's something I did before my relationship and continue to do to this day. This meant I had to ask my partner if she was comfortable with me continuing.

You'll also need to explain the ramifications with your partner. If they aren't comfortable with you having sleepovers with friends of any gender, and that is something you regularly do, that's going to impact on your friendships. If your friends suddenly feel that you've changed since going into a relationship, and that certain things that were normal are now weird, it will put them at odds with your partner. That said, friends, no matter how comfortable we are with them, need to be accommodating of your new relationship and expect that some things might change.

Having to establish where the line is with each new partner, and it being so clearly influenced by cultural conditioning about sexuality, can be frustrating for bi people, particularly when we feel a partner is being patronizing, believing that we can't control ourselves in the presence of other people and will be instantly consumed by passion. I do feel bi people are more attuned to what they want sexually, and if they've made a commitment, they will stick to it. To then be told that you have to adhere to all of these ridiculous safeguarding techniques to ensure you aren't tempted can cause arguments. At the end of the day, if you're going to cheat, you're going to cheat. They can't keep you locked away in the basement.

This can be a tricky topic to manage and cataclysmic if you get it wrong. I again urge you to be open with your partner and discuss upfront where the lines are.

SEX

**I've only ever had sex with men. How should
I approach my first time with a woman?**

Your first time with a new gender is bound to be a steady
mix of excitement and pure terror. Take it slow and don't
put pressure on yourself.

The trickier thing about having sex with women compared with having sex with men is that the man is often
expected to lead. Of course, this isn't always the case, but
you might want to prepare yourself for being expected to
take charge of the action. If you have had sex with men
before, this shouldn't be too hard. Either you're used to
taking the lead or you've been on the receiving end of
men taking the lead. Either of these experiences will give
you more than enough knowledge to know what to do.

Obviously, a woman's body is very different to a man's.
I'm afraid this isn't going to be a graphic step-by-step

guide on what to do. What I will do is encourage you to have a play. This woman clearly likes you and is willing to have sex with you. So get with the programme, go ahead and explore her body. See what makes her tingle and moan with pleasure. If you're enjoying yourself and relaxed, then hopefully she will be too.

With women, gentle touch and sustained activity tends to be better than the aggressive and fast-paced tempo some men like to keep. But do ask your partner what feels good, ask them if they like it like that and tell them to describe their fantasies to you. Sex should be fun, not something we're ashamed of, feel the need to rush or overthink.

If you are a woman, then rely on the experiences of your own body. What has felt good to you before? Do that! Think of yourself as having an advantage here: you have the same body parts, so do everything you've always wanted someone to do to you – with their consent, of course. Your first same-sex experience is bound to be daunting, but you've most probably waited long enough for it, so enjoy yourself. Also, be kind to yourself and set low expectations; maybe it will be embarrassing and she won't get off – so what? It's important to take the pressure off yourself and just explore.

I've only ever had sex with women. How should I approach my first time with a man?

If you're a man who's used to sex with women and are

now considering your first time with a man, there are a few key differences to think about.

Between a man and a woman, the positions are well defined. The majority of the time, the man leads and he's the one to penetrate. When you're having sex with someone of the same gender, these roles go out the window.

I'd encourage you to think in advance about what you're comfortable with for the first time. Will this be just oral? Are you okay with penetrating him? Are you okay with him penetrating you?

I'd encourage you to discuss with your partner beforehand what they like to do in bed so that you can prepare and make sure you're comfortable. One thing to consider about gay sex is that it can't always be spontaneous as there is usually some prep work involved. For example, if you are going to be penetrated, it's strongly advised that you douche to make sure everything is clean. If this is your first time, you might also want to consider poppers that can help relax you. I should, of course, mention that neither of these are essential – it's about what works for you. Poppers aren't for everyone, and douching too much is dangerous, so always do your research first or talk with friends if you're unsure. My final tip here is, for his sake, go on top the first time; this will allow you to be in control of the penetration and make sure things are happening at a speed that suits you.

If you are a bi woman having your first experience with a man, then that advice is doubled. Being penetrated by a penis is a deeply intimate and sometimes invasive thing to have happen. If you've got used to being in a same-sex sexual relationship, then having that dynamic change can feel overwhelming. Suddenly, there is a body part that wasn't in the equation before. I'm going to assume that if you're reading this question, then you do want the experience, but as with bi men, it is about making sure that you are comfortable and have an open discussion. You also need to think about birth control ahead of time. A lot of bisexuals who are in same-sex relationships forget about having to worry about unexpected pregnancies, but if you're a bi woman having sex with a guy, then you do need to think about how you're going to prevent this. This comes down to personal choice, but if you decide he needs to wear a condom, then be firm in your decision and make it clear that sex is not happening without it. Having a man 'take the lead' in sex can also be daunting, even if it is just him being in charge of the tempo of thrusting. Sex is a skill, so the more you do it, the more you will feel comfortable; go at your own speed and don't feel rushed or pressured.

Is it wrong that I don't like to use condoms with women?

This issue is one of the great under-examined areas of the bisexual experience. Are we more or less likely to use protection based on the sex of the person we are having intercourse with? Over the years, a lot of bi men have raised this issue with me, and I would say a common attitude seems to be always using a condom with a man but not as much with a woman. There are several reasons I've been given for this. Some bi men state that the STI risk of having sex with another man is higher than with a woman. Others feel anal sex can be messy, and they'd rather that mess was on a condom. Similarly, some men just feel vaginas are cleaner and designed for a penis, so feel better about going in bare.

Equally, I've heard the complete opposite: that now so many gay and bi men are on PrEP, sex with men is safer and it's women getting pregnant that bi men need to worry about.

I've also heard some alarming views too – such as it being a woman's responsibility to make sure she doesn't get pregnant. Some have even found the impregnation risk with a woman a thrill – which, of course, it isn't. Bringing a baby into the world isn't a fetish.

On the flip side, with bi women, some may be more cautious about safe sex with men because of the pregnancy risk but take a more relaxed attitude with other women.

The truth is, bisexuals with bad condom practices are a result of sexual health campaigns forgetting we are there. That said, you should be using condoms with all your sexual partners regardless of their genitals. The risks may differ based on gender and sex, but all forms of intercourse have risk.

So, to answer the question, it is wrong that you aren't using condoms. If you prefer sex without condoms, you need to be either in a monogamous relationship or ensure both you and a partner are clear of infections beforehand.

I'm scared of being judged at the sexual health clinic. Do I have to tell them about my bisexuality?

Coming out to a healthcare provider is a big step for many bisexuals. I remember spending years giving fake names at clinics because I was terrified there would be a medical record and 'proof' of my bisexual exploits.

It feels like a very official way of documenting your sexuality, which can be incredibly daunting. If you have a similar view, you're in good company. Research by the Equality Network found that only 33 per cent of bisexuals usually feel comfortable and 28 per cent never feel comfortable sharing their sexual orientation with their general practitioner (Rankin *et al.*, 2015).

Unfortunately for bisexuals, finding the courage to come out to a healthcare provider isn't the end of the story. Many healthcare providers are clueless when it comes to bisexuality, and it's not uncommon for them to harbour their own prejudice. The London Assembly Health Committee documented this, finding that bisexual people, and those who come under the + category, report that their identity is frequently misunderstood or simply erased by health professionals (London Assembly Health Committee, 2017).

I have been on the receiving end of people who work in sexual health clinics letting themselves down when it comes to bisexual care. I remember one woman looking at me as if I'd just told her aliens built the pyramids, as I detailed the mix of men and women I'd had sex with since my last check-up.

I also once took issue with a healthcare worker trying to give me a leaflet on gay sexual health. When I asked if I could have one specific to bi men's health, I was told the gay leaflet covered it – which, of course, it didn't. It said nothing about pregnancy risk.

The answer to the question on this one is no. You don't have to tell the sexual health clinic about your bisexuality, but it's much better for everyone if you do.

First, it's better for you. It means you'll be checked for all the relevant infections you might have caught. It means you don't have the stress of lying, remembering the stories you told and inventing situations that didn't happen to justify why you need to be checked for specific infections.

Second, it's good for the health services. There is already an issue with the way they approach bi care. If we are going to pretend to be gay or straight when accessing services, how on earth are they going to learn?

We need to be visible, and they need to see our disappointed little faces when they tell us they don't have a leaflet on bisexuality. They need to feel that urge to better themselves and get up to speed on bisexuality.

The reality is we need to be going further than just coming out to them. We need to be leaving negative or positive reviews of the service we receive to let them know the bisexuals are watching and that their performance in the space is not going unnoticed.

If you feel strong enough, this is an area where you can help. Many bisexuals will be deterred from coming out to healthcare providers, so it's up to the rest of us to push for better services, to make ourselves visible and hold services accountable. What we want is for healthcare providers to take some responsibility and make sure they overcompensate to make bisexual people feel welcome and safe.

We shouldn't be scared about coming out to sexual healthcare providers – it's their bloody job. If they're shocked that some people have sex with more than one gender, it might be time to get the career adviser on the phone because something has gone terribly wrong.

This issue isn't just about their comfort; it's about yours too. Ideally, you should be working yourself up to a place where you are comfortable with your sexuality and no one can shame you for it. Why should you be ashamed that you're bisexual and clearly in demand? You shouldn't be embarrassed; this should be a victory lap. 'Yes, all these people wanted to sleep with me. Yes, they all orgasmed. Yes, they all wanted to come back for a second round. And, yes, we used protection but you can never be too careful.'

I want to have a biological child. Is it wrong to choose to be with a woman/man simply because of this?

This is a tricky one to give an answer to, yet it's one of the most common questions bi people ask. It might come as a shock this far into the book that bi people do have other interests and priorities outside of being bisexual – but it's true.

Many people out there want to have children, and that is considerably easier to achieve if you are in a couple with opposite sets of genitals. For gay men and lesbians, it's tough luck. Very early on in their journeys, they have to accept that a biological child with the person they love isn't scientifically possible yet (unless, of course, they have a trans partner). This allows them time to explore other options such as surrogacy and adoption.

For bi people, it can seem like we have a choice. If you are someone who wants children, then ending up with a partner of the opposite sex will usually mean you'll have an easier time.

But is this using someone? Is this being a dishonest bisexual? The answer is yes, no and maybe. It's really hard to tell because bisexuality is different for everyone. Some bisexuals may be more attracted to the opposite sex than same sex, in which case baby-making capacity is just an added bonus. For other bisexuals, their dominant attraction may be to the same sex – possibly, they don't feel much in the way of romantic feelings towards the opposite sex – but they are planning to force it in order to have biological children. This I would frown upon unless their partner was completely aware of these feelings and was okay with it.

Morally, this is tricky, and the truth is, you'll know yourself if what you are doing is right or wrong. Believe it or not, though, bisexuals are only human, and we can't be expected to make moral decisions all the time. And let's not forget here that some very loved-up straight people end up breaking up because one of them can't have a child. There are sufficient arguments both in favour and against, so much so that delving into the discussion of what is right and wrong on this issue could easily fill an entire book. This is such an emotive issue and a deal breaker for many, so we won't be held to higher standards just because we are bisexual.

I'd also bring this back to my belief that you can't go into your sexuality with a game plan. If you're attracted to more than one gender, and you embrace that and go out into the world looking for a life partner, there is just no way to guarantee the sex or genitals of the person you're going to end up with. If, for example, you're a bi woman and you wanted to end up with a guy for children, are you really going to turn away a woman if the chemistry, sex and love between you is off the charts? I hope not.

Whatever your decision here, just make sure your partner is aware. Ten bisexual points for not making them feel as though they were just the sperm or egg you needed to fulfil your breeding plan.

MENTAL HEALTH

I feel so isolated. How can I make some bisexual friends?

I often find that bi people can be among some of the most isolated people of all the sexual minorities. It's important here to recognize why bi people run into each other so infrequently.

First, we are the only sexuality that regularly dates outside of our orientation. What I mean is that when it comes to gay people, for example, they usually date other gay people. Taking gay men as an example, yes, they do also have the option of bi men, but gay men dating other gay men is by far the most common scenario. As gay men, they can't afford to not meet other people who share their sexual orientation. If they don't, they aren't going to have sex or find love. Hence the gay clubs, hook-up spots and dating apps.

Bisexual people aren't bound by such rules. We can date gay people, straight people and other bi people, so the need to meet other bi people just hasn't existed in the way it would have if we were bound by only being able to find love and sex with other bi people.

As we see with the gay bars and apps, while a huge motivation behind their creation might have been finding a partner, a consequence is that it also created culture and friendships. You may have to kiss a lot of frogs to find your prince, and some of those frogs or just people you meet along the way can become great friends.

The second factor explaining why bi people can feel isolated is that just because they meet other bisexuals, it doesn't mean they will have much in common. Sticking with our comparison of gay men, they often have things in common: attractions towards men, the stigma they face, issues with sex, politics on dating apps, etc. Bi people tend not to have universal experiences: they might be bi but have only ever dated women, they might be a virgin, trans, etc. Their level of 'outness' might also be different, with some being out to everyone they know and others out to just a few close confidants.

Another issue I've personally encountered is that of bisexuals viewing each other as a threat. You have to understand that many out bi people have been setting their own rules for years. They've had to single-handedly deal with biphobia, explain how bisexuality works to their nearest and dearest, and figure out how their bisexuality fits into their life. Another bisexual coming along can feel threatening. What if they have a different take? What if you've been telling those closest to you that bisexuals can be monogamous and then another bi comes along to tell them it's impossible?

Early on after my coming out, I remember encountering another bi man. I was at an event, and someone mentioned that one of the other guys there was, like me, a bi man. I was instantly excited – finally, someone like me, someone who understood. I had to say hello. After working up some courage and waiting for him to be alone, I made my approach. My mind has blocked out most of what happened next but, needless to say, it didn't go well. He basically ridiculed me and told me I wasn't bisexual; it was just that I hadn't realized I was gay yet. To say I felt downtrodden was an understatement. As human beings, we generally like to connect with people who share our experiences – from people who grew up in our hometown that we bump into while out in the city, to those who support the same sports team. And especially sexuality.

Worse, my negative first experience turned out to be a trailer for the full movie. I've been involved in bisexual activism for more than six years. In that time, I've really tried to push bisexual issues into the mainstream, writing articles for national news organizations, appearing on television and even debating the infamous Piers Morgan. In that time, the hardest criticism to take hasn't come from biphobic gay men or sceptical straights. It's been other bi people. Bi people who had read my article or watched my interview and disagreed. They felt I didn't represent their views, that my anger at the lack of funding from LGBTQ+ groups was misplaced, or that in pointing out the neglect bi people face, I'd actually erased some of the work other bisexuals were doing. It was hard for me to accept that there wasn't a harmonious bisexual experience or take on bisexuality; that bisexuals tend to be so different that it's hard for many of them to agree on things.

I explain these elements as part cautionary tale and part managing your expectations. Go out there and find other bisexuals to be friends with; they'll be some of the best friendships you'll have. But just as with dating, it probably won't be instantaneous and you might have to go on some bad dates to find the right people. You also need to remember that bi people aren't just bisexual. You might have a few interesting conversations around bisexuality, but you're going to need to connect on a much deeper level than that if your friendship is going to stand the test of time.

This was part of my motivation for joining the Bisexual Brunch podcast as a co-host. It allows us to have bi-focused conversations that many bi people don't get to have because they know so few bi people. We get to go in deep on topics that you just can't do in a 1000-word article or a three-minute TV debate. There are also three of us who all have different takes on whatever it is that we are talking about.

In my experience, a great way to find other bi people is to get online. There are lots of bi people you could connect with who tend to be posting bi-specific content and having bi-focused discussions. You could easily slide into their DMs and get a friendship growing.

If you're looking for more of a face-to-face connection, many major cities have local bi meet-up groups. A little online research should reveal when the next appropriate event is. I'd always suggest taking an outgoing friend with you (they don't need to be bi) to make you feel more comfortable and not completely alone.

There are also ways to lure other bisexuals to you in LGBTQ+ settings. I've gone to various Prides and gay bars wearing a bisexual T-shirt. This approach works every time and allows other bisexuals in the building to find you. Always keep an eye out for that one person who keeps looking at you but seems to lack the confidence to come over and say hi.

Ultimately, while you shouldn't give up trying, do your best to not let the lack of bi people in your life get you down. A report by the Equality Network found that 85 per cent of bi people do not feel part of a bisexual community (Rankin *et al.*, 2015). So, if you feel you do have supportive bi people around you, count yourselves lucky – you're in the minority.

It's terrifying to not even know the gender of the person I'm going to end up with. How do I deal with the uncertainty?

As we explored in the previous chapter, being bisexual creates a huge amount of uncertainty as so much of our experience can be dictated by the gender of our partners.

The truth is, with uncertainty, the only way out is through. You have to embrace your path and enjoy the ride. Yes, the uncertainty is unique, but most people deal with uncertainty about the future.

Even straight people who might take being able to have biological children at some point in the future for granted could end up with someone who can't have children.

As bi people, we can get in our heads about the uncertainty because we have a false sense that we have lots of options. The biphobic stigma is that bisexuals are attracted to everyone or that we have more choice than most. Well, let's play out that analogy a little...

Think of streaming platforms – thousands of films and TV shows to watch, whenever, wherever. This often isn't a good thing. We can spend hours choosing something to watch and then end up not actually having enough time to finish it before bed. If, like me, you remember a simpler time where there were only five TV channels, everything was a lot less stressful. Making a decision was quicker, and putting up with a plot that you weren't that interested in was something you'd do.

There is also a concept I'm fond of called the 'paradox of choice'. It's the idea that too much choice has a negative impact on our mental health. Sticking with our TV analogy, back when there were only five channels, if you couldn't find anything to watch, it wasn't your fault. If you did end up watching a film and didn't like it, it was the TV channel's fault for putting it on. Now, streaming giants have put so many choices at our fingertips, if you can't find something to watch, clearly it's your fault. If you watch a film and didn't love it, it's your fault. Too much choice can cause paralysis in decision making. It also puts more responsibility on us to make the right choice for fear of feeling like we've failed.

Bisexuals need to be careful not to fall into this trap. In life, as with the streaming platforms, it feels as if we have a lot of choice when it comes to gender and people of different sexualities. A relationship with a gay man/lesbian is going to be different to a relationship with a trans woman/trans man, as would a relationship with another bi man/bi woman. Bisexuals can feel lost. If they settle down with one person, it feels as though they are closing the doors on the many thousands of different futures they could have had with people from different walks of life. On the flip side, they aren't getting any younger and might worry they'll die alone if they don't find 'the one' soon.

There is no correct answer to this question. There is just a warning to not be in your own head about all the 'choice' and possibilities that come with your bisexuality. Get out there and meet people, and don't worry too much about the ramifications or tomorrow. An asteroid could hit the planet at any second anyway. Just be open and the right person will come along, and when they do, you'll know – you'll feel the spark. And I'll bet they weren't who you thought you'd end up with.

With my fiancée, I remember meeting her and knowing instantly she was the one. Since we are among friends, I'll tell you the truth, when I met her, I thought, 'Fuck!'

I'd only been single for six months at the time and was having all the slutty bisexual fun you could imagine. I wasn't looking for a relationship. But I knew there and then that I couldn't let her get away. She was perfect. She also probably wasn't who I would have gone for on paper. She had a child from a previous relationship which meant becoming a step-parent. Not something I thought I would have ever done before meeting her, but something that has turned out to be an enriching experience.

Embrace the path, bisexuals. Don't fear it.

Do you think my bisexuality makes me appear as less manly?

Dating as a bisexual man can be very tricky waters to navigate. According to a survey conducted among bisexual men (around 3000 Taimi users), over 92 per cent stated that bisexual men face significant challenges or difficulties in dating and relationships with heterosexual women (Taimi, 2023).

This isn't just about tone of voice or mannerisms for many bi men, it can feel like they are competing with straight men for women's attention and that their 'gay past' is a negative thing to bring to the table. Gay men don't have this pressure; not appearing 'conventionally masculine' doesn't hinder their dating prospects in the same way.

I'd *love* to say here that someone who needs you to be displaying your masculinity or would see feminine traits in a male as undesirable isn't worth your time. But this book is about real bisexuals, in the real world, living real lives and interacting with real people. Of fucking course how a man displays his masculinity matters to a huge portion of women.

Research from the *Journal of Bisexuality* found that straight women perceived bi men as being less romantically and sexually attractive than straight men. As a result, straight women were less likely to date or have sex with a bi guy. Bi men were also perceived as being significantly more feminine than straight men (Gleason *et al.*, 2018).

If you're a single male bisexual open to dating women, this is going to be something you encounter and something you're going to have to manage. I truly believe the lack of women open to dating bisexual men is why so many of us are still closeted, so tackling this issue is crucial to moving our people forward.

Let's get back to the matter at hand. Does being bisexual make you less 'manly'? I mean, what is manly? Everyone's definition is going to be different. Does it mean that your penis is going to be smaller than a straight man's? Well, that's defo not true. Does it mean you're going to fuck less well than a more manly straight man? Defo not – in my experience, bi men fuck better. Does it mean you won't be a good father, provider, fighter? No.

The truth is there is no substance in the notion that being bisexual makes you less of a man. It's really about you as a person. Maybe you do have a more feminine voice or interests. Try not to be with someone who would see that as a negative thing. That said, too many bisexual men see their sexuality as a hindrance in appearing masculine enough to attract a woman. So, what can be done?

The first thing I'd say is know your facts. There has been a study that came out very positively for women who were in relationships with bisexual men. The Deakin School of Health and Social Development interviewed 78 Australian women who were in relationships with bisexual men. They found that overall these women felt their bisexual partners were better lovers and fathers than straight men (Williams, 2016). Some women even said they would never be able to go back to dating heterosexual men at all. It turned out that straight men were the ones with more emotional and misogynistic baggage. Overall, the women felt that bi men were far more respectful and wanted to set up equitable gender relationships in the home.

The second thing I'd say is lean into being bisexual. If you act apologetic or see it as a hindrance, how are you going to convince other people that there is nothing wrong with it? It's on you to sell your bisexuality and your masculinity, to walk with confidence with both and make people feel as though they're missing out on something by dismissing you.

Bisexuals are travelling in the direction of becoming a majority. If all of us do our bit to sell it with style, make people see it in a good way, we will shift the dial from people seeing bisexuality as a drawback to it being something coveted, something people are envious of. Check your history books. Masculinity, and what is considered to be masculine, is always changing. There's no reason we can't make bisexual men be seen as one of the most masculine things to be.

Now that I'm in a 'straight-facing' relationship, my queer friends have gone back to calling me straight, and I'm tired of arguing with them. How do I get them to take my sexuality and my relationship seriously?

It's not uncommon for friends to see your current relationship as proof that they were right all along – that you are in fact gay/straight.

This sloppy and silly comment can be voiced from time to time, and you will need to put people in their box.

Usually, a simple explanation will be enough: that, just like them, you still have attractions to people outside of your current relationship but choose not to act on it. Just as their hormones didn't die the day they met their partner, neither did yours.

It's also fair to explain why you're calling out the comment – that suggesting your sexuality is determined by the gender of your partner is offensive. It's something bisexuals are told all too often by straight and gay people who haven't got a clue, and you find it distasteful.

However, sometimes these comments can become a recurring issue. If so, it might be time to take a slightly firmer line when dealing with it.

My favourite approach here is actually to just shout at them. They're your friends and they should know better, especially if you've already taken the time to explain how it works. Why not try something along the lines of:

> Could I just say that your comments about me being straight are actually fucking annoying me now. The fact that you think my sexuality has changed because I'm dating someone that happens to be X gender just shows how ignorant you are. I'm actually embarrassed for you that you don't get such a simple concept. If you don't have anything interesting to say about my sexuality, then can you just keep your mouth shut because I'm tired of hearing your nonsense.

Obviously, we aren't all so blatantly confrontational. Some of us might want to approach the topic with a little joke. Something along the lines of 'Trust me, I'm still bisexual. If Megan Fox shows up, my new man is old news.'

If you choose the jokey approach, I would caution that there is only so long you should spend trying to convince a friend to hear you on this topic. If they continue to push this narrative that your bisexuality is over and you've made your choice, it's a sign something is wrong.

It's possible that they like you romantically, and this is their way of dealing with it. Perhaps they're just biphobic and it's time to end the friendship. Whatever the reason, don't suffer being undermined for too long. While only you will know the best way to deal with your friend, I can tell you that a good friend wouldn't use your bisexuality as a weapon to attack you.

What does success as a bi person look like?

For many of us, having an end goal or a vision of what a perfect future looks like is essential for figuring out what we define as successful. Outside of sexuality, people might say getting to the top of the career ladder, getting married or having children. It can help to have a similar outlook when it comes to your sexuality, particularly if you're at a stage in your life where you aren't out to everyone yet or you still have some nervousness around bisexuality yourself.

This will differ for everyone, and different people will have different visions of success and what a harmonious future looks like, but there are some common themes I've heard from speaking to bisexual people over the years.

The first is self-acceptance. That, in the future, you'll walk with confidence as a bi person. Any negative comments you receive won't hurt you because you've finally, truly embraced your bisexuality. You know for a fact that anyone with an issue is wrong and dealing with their own unhappiness and suffering from their small-minded view of the world. They no longer possess the power to bring you down or make you question yourself.

Tied to this is the idea of finally being out to everyone. That there is no one in your life who you feel like you couldn't tell about your bisexuality for fear of rejection or discrimination.

Let's not forget that, for some bisexuals, privacy is key. Success might be getting to achieve their goals outside of their sexuality and feeling that their sexuality did not in any way hinder their achievement.

Some bisexuals will feel success by helping other bi people. They may envision a future where they help to form or grow bisexual communities. Similarly, they may focus on making sure bi voices are heard and that LGBTQ+ groups better serve us.

For some, success as a bisexual might come down to sex itself. Maybe you want to have every sexual experience under the rainbow of bisexual possibilities. All the genders, all the positions, all the sex parties. As long as everyone is consenting and safe, good luck to you and have fun.

Many may also see success in terms of being able to manage their attractions; of understanding if a monogamous relationship works for them and, if so, how to have an outlet for their attractions outside of their partner, if they need to. Others may accept that monogamy is not for them, and therefore success lies in finding a non-monogamous situation that suits all those involved. Some may not be interested in finding a life partner, choosing instead to be single and having casual relationships that work for them.

For many, though, success in the bisexual journey is finding that special person or persons to spend your life with – having a committed relationship with a certain someone who not only accepts you but celebrates you. A person who awakens your life and helps you to be the best version of yourself.

THE COMMUNITY

A new bisexual has entered my friendship group and they are invalidating my perception of bisexuality. What do I do?

As we've already explored in this book, sometimes another bisexual coming along isn't always a jumping-for-joy experience. In fact, sometimes it can be quite scary.

If a new bisexual person has entered your life and you're starting to feel that they're challenging your perception of what it means to be bisexual, there are a few things you can do.

The first thing is to talk to them. So, you disagree on a few things. Why not find out the areas of the bisexual experience that you do agree on? Maybe you feel the same about bisexual people needing more attention from LGBTQ+ groups. Maybe you're both passionate about being more visible as bi people. Have a few of these topics in your head and, when the moment is right, bring them up and see if you can get a discussion going. If you can, work out the areas you agree on, then you can always circle back to them if the conversations around bisexuality go to a topic you don't want to discuss.

Second, you're going to have to make peace with the idea that no two bisexuals are the same and that's okay. Enjoy hearing their perspectives and feel free to push back if you really don't agree with something they are saying. Often, when it comes to bisexuality, because it's an issue we've been struggling with, it can be packed with emotion and feel exaggerated. Try to take those feelings away if you can. Imagine you're discussing the rules of your favourite sport instead.

Why is bisexuality so dismissed by LGBTQ+ groups?

Bisexuals can have a complicated relationship with the LGBTQ+ community. Some bisexuals won't have a problem at all and will find various groups and organizations to be helpful, but many of us do have issues with the status quo.

It really depends on what you see the LGBTQ+ community as being there to do. If you feel it's a simple matter-of-fact entity, where minorities have banded together to help each other, you might not feel that there is a problem. If you see it as a bunch of organizations that have elected themselves to be in charge of our care, and you feel they're doing a bad job of it, you might very well have something negative to say.

To give you a flavour of how bisexual people tend to feel about the LGBTQ+ community, the Equality Network found that 66 per cent of bisexuals only felt 'a little' or 'not at all' part of the LGBT community (Rankin *et al.*, 2015). When looking at why this might be the case, it's even more confusing when we consider the demographics. Research has found bisexuals make up 52 per cent of all LGB people (GLAAD, 2016).

That's right, when it comes to numbers, we're actually the majority, and that, really, is where a lot of the issues come from. Many bisexual people feel that, as a majority, the LGBTQ+ movement should be doing much more to support bi people. Yet, as things stand, it's easy for a bisexual person to feel underrepresented and deprioritized in the movement.

Nowhere is this truer than when we look at the funding.

Tracking the funding for bisexual people, or the LGBTQ+ community at large, is not an easy task. Many groups, charities and organizations don't disclose how much money they have and even fewer tell us how they spend their funds by identity.

One of the best indicators of how much funding is invested in the specific identities of the LGBTQ+ community can be found in the work conducted by Funders for LGBTQ+ Issues. The organization tracks LGBTQ+ grant making by both US foundations and international institutions. It produces an annual tracking report and other special reports to monitor the character of LGBTQ+ funding and identify trends, gaps and opportunities.

One of the most telling reports the organization published was its 'Forty years of LGBTQ philanthropy 1970–2010'. It documented the first 40 years of US foundation support to lesbian, gay, bisexual, transgender and queer communities. The report details LGBTQ+ grant making by sexual orientation, gender identity and sex characteristics. The report found that bisexuals receive disproportionately little financial support from philanthropic organizations – less than 0.1 per cent of the overall funding. The numbers show that bisexuals only received $84,000 between 1970 and 2010 compared with gay men who received $34,173,243 (Bowen, 2012).

If you're wondering if the situation has improved in the 13 years since that report, you're in for a disappointment. At the time of writing, the 2019–2020 tracking report, released in 2022, provides the most up-to-date figures. There was just $58,333 spent on bisexual people in 2020, less than allies ($1,343,434), and far, far, far less than the $9,386,675 spent on gay men (note, the term 'gay men' is expanded in this most recent report to include gay men/queer men/MSM) (Lawther *et al.*, 2022).

Although we don't have the same figures available in the UK, we don't need to call in Jessica Fletcher or Columbo. You can see for yourself how often specific bisexual services, events and resources are on offer. If we make up half the movement, does it really feel like we are getting half the focus? Do we feel that issues that specifically impact bisexual people are ever focused on? How many of these groups, charities and organizations, which have elected themselves in charge of our care, could competently explain how they are supporting bi people and how that support differs from the support they provide to gay men or lesbians?

Groups often try to get around the fact that they don't make any real effort to support bi people by saying they support all queer people. In my opinion, one of the biggest problems with the LGBTQ+ movement is this amalgamation. The idea that unity is best.

When it comes to a poster or a rallying cry, yes, of course, unity among all queer people is better – standing together, protecting each other and making sure no one is left behind. The problem is, that doesn't really work practically when it comes to actually improving the lives of queer people.

For example, one of the issues that really gets my back up is the way in which sexual health research is conducted. Despite my best efforts, gay and bisexual men are often viewed together under the same microscope. This means we often get health figures that have absolutely no basis in reality and, in my opinion, aren't worth the paper they are written on. For example, a few years back, Public Health England put out a report that found sexually transmitted diseases had increased by 10 per cent in Britain's gay and bisexual men (Hayes, 2016). This was designed to be informative and drive positive change, with its amalgamation of gay and bi men standard practice.

This is where I say amalgamation is the problem. Gay and bi men, by nature, have different sex lives. Gay men typically only sleep with men. Bi men could be sleeping with men and women. Taking this joint approach basically means only the issues bi men face that also exist for gay men are ever looked at. Sexual health research so often won't look at bi people's risk of pregnancy or how being bisexual impacts on their attitude towards pregnancy. To my knowledge, there has never even been any research to ask bi people if they are more likely to use a condom with a man or a woman.

It's not just sexual health but health reports in general that seem not to be able to distinguish between gay and bi people. Take, for example, a study conducted by the London School of Hygiene and Tropical Medicine and funded by Stonewall, the LGBTQ+ charity. The study revealed that gay or bisexual men aged 26 or under are twice as likely to suffer from anxiety or depression and six times as likely to have attempted suicide as men aged 45 or over (Lees, 2016).

The problem here, yet again, is that the study doesn't distinguish between gay and bi men. Are bi men just as likely as gay men to attempt suicide or is there a difference? Are gay men suicidal because people keep telling them their sexuality is a phase too? Are gay men depressed because gay men won't date them? (And, no, that's not a typo: many straight women won't date bi men, and that has an impact.) If these nuances are lost and researchers and LGBTQ+ groups don't understand that a gay person is different from a bi person, then they have no business being in charge of our care.

The problem is that key issues that impact certain areas of the LGBTQ+ community are ignored. As a consequence, if we don't know something is happening, we can't look to find solutions. As I mentioned, coming out as a bi man can make you less attractive to straight and gay people. This doesn't happen for gay men: coming out as gay doesn't make you less attractive to gay men. As there is no correlation, the issue remains unexamined and untackled by the LGBTQ+ community.

The 'if it doesn't happen to gay men, it doesn't happen' attitude drives bisexuals like me crazy and makes me question the point of this collaborative approach to improving the lives of queer people. Some bisexuals go much further than me and feel that bisexuals are being robbed and extorted. Some people in the bisexual community resent donating to causes that are meant to help all LGBTQ+ people but in reality favour particular sexualities and keep bisexual funding back in the 1970s.

This brings us nicely to the other issue with the LGBTQ+ community – internal biphobia and the reality that many gay men and lesbians don't believe in bisexuality.

There's actually a term for it – the 'androcentric desire hypothesis'. Researchers came up with it to describe the phenomenon they observed of gay and lesbian people perceiving bisexuals as being more attracted to men. This perception means bisexuals are viewed negatively and are defined by their attractions towards men, with bi women seen as really being straight and lying, and bi men seen as being gay and lying.

This attitude hasn't gone unnoticed. A report by the Equality Network in 2015 found that the highest incidents of biphobia experienced are within LGBTQ+ services and NHS services (Rankin *et al.*, 2015). Similarly, Stonewall found 27 per cent of bi women and 18 per cent of bi men have experienced biphobia from within the LGBTQ+ community (Glass, 2018).

Herein lies the problem. If a significant number of gay and lesbian people think bisexuality isn't a thing, they can make sure that our issues don't get given the time of day and that we don't receive a penny of funding. Why would they waste their time on something they don't believe in?

You also have to factor in the gay and lesbian people in positions of power in the LGBTQ+ community who do believe we exist but don't think that our suffering is anywhere near as bad as theirs, and that the resource and time they could spend on bi people could be put to use elsewhere. These people often reason that any issues we face from the straight world will be dealt with there and any issues we experience because of our same-sex attractions will be sorted because of the work being done in the queer community.

Gay men and women by and large run the LGBTQ+ scene; there is not a massive representation of bi, pan or trans people in positions of power in queer organizations, and it is past time this changed.

How do we improve the LGBTQ+ community for bi people?

As bisexual people, once we understand some of the shortcomings of the LGBTQ+ community, it's natural to wonder how we could fix it.

In my experience, there are numerous ways to add your power to effect change; it's just a matter of deciding what role you want to have.

You could start by spreading the word – a lot of people have no idea that bisexuals aren't equally represented or cared for by the LGBTQ+ community. Being able to competently and confidently explain the situation to other people goes a long way. It increases the number of people aware of the situation who will have it in the back of their minds the next time they deal with queer community issues.

Speak truth to power. It's important to put our points to those in positions of power in the LGBTQ+ community. They need to know that we see what they are doing and that there is discontent with the amount of focus bisexual people are receiving. I've done this a lot in my time as a bisexual activist. Whenever I meet anyone from any LGBTQ+ organization, the first thing I ask is what they are doing for bisexual people specifically. Often, they try to fob me off with things they are doing for the queer community as a whole. It's important to push past this and ask again what specifically they are doing. Regardless of their answer, you should give your observations of the areas where you think LGBTQ+ organizations could serve the bisexual community better. This ensures that when they next get back to the office, they know that they need to start having a better track record as an organization on bisexuality.

It's easy to think of LGBTQ+ organizations as these huge powerful entities, but the truth is they are run by everyday human beings, and human beings can be persuaded. If everyone reading this book has these conversations with people in power, they will feel the atmosphere change and it will shift the dial.

The final answer to this question is to have a seat at the table. The best thing we can do is have a position of influence within these organizations. No matter how big or small – maybe it's just the local LGBTQ+ group or society at your college or university – sitting at the table as decisions are being made and making sure that bisexual voices are heard is beyond important.

How do I deal with a gay man who doesn't believe in bisexuality because it was a phase for him?

For those of you that haven't experienced this issue, believe me, it's coming. It usually involves a man who identifies as gay questioning another male's bisexuality. The basis for this is that the gay guy himself identified as bisexual on the way out of the closet, and so believes that all bisexuals must be doing the same. It's worth pointing out that I am, of course, not talking about all gay men here, but it's happened often enough to me that I would assume most bisexuals are going to run into this issue.

This situation can throw you terribly because it can seem to us, and probably any spectators listening in, that the gay guy is the wiser one. It's completely invalidating and really hard to defend against. They are basically saying, 'I was where you are and it's complete nonsense. Learn from my mistakes.'

This is by far one of the most infuriating issues I've personally run into. Gay men identifying as bisexual on the way out of the closet is a big factor in why people think bisexuality is a phase. Bi people didn't create that stigma; gay men who first identified as bisexual did. For those people to not then be sympathetic but actually to enforce the stigma they created is a very hard pill to swallow, as well as being something no one wants to talk about.

This behaviour should never be excused, and when you encounter this attitude, the first step is to wrestle back the power. In this situation, the gay man sees you as his past; he feels you are an infant in your understanding of sexuality in comparison with him who is at the finish line. You need to establish that he is the one with closed-minded views and that you understand and have dealt with this situation before.

Personally, I'm all for being really blunt here: something

along the lines of, 'Oh joy, another gay guy that doesn't believe in bisexuality. How original!'

Once you knock them off their 'know it all' pedestal, it's time to educate them so that they *never* subject another bi person to their prejudice again.

I usually explain that it is gay men who have created the 'bi now, gay tomorrow' myth, and that rather than enforcing the stigma, it would be more helpful for them to think about how they can heal this damage and create more bi-visibility in the world.

It's probably worth pointing out that this issue is, of course, a taboo topic. No one wants to discuss it, and no one wants to take responsibility for it being a thing. Although I advocate not letting biphobic gay men get away with this attitude, we must be slightly sensitive at the same time.

The truth is, no one should have to come out. It's a horrid and often traumatic process that exists because society assumes everyone is straight. For some gay men, identifying as bisexual on the way out of the closet made the whole process easier. It possibly helped them, in their own mind, to cope with the idea that they didn't like women, that they wouldn't have biological children and that having sex with men was okay if they also had sex with women. Externally, it also helped them test the waters with those around them. Would they accept them as bi? Is it less bad than gay? Was it easier with their parents to kill the idea of grandkids slowly rather than with a quick fatal blow?

It's for these reasons that I am sympathetic to why some gay men find it easier to come out as bi first. I think we have to be in a position where we acknowledge that gay men doing this hurts bisexual men's credibility and is the reason for the stigma, but still arrive at a place where we say that we don't judge anyone's coming-out journey.

The line must firmly be drawn, however, when gay men use this journey to purposely hurt bi men.

There is actually a study that was conducted on this issue. Granted, it was a limited study, but, as I mentioned above, no one wants to look at this issue and LGBTQ+ groups certainly aren't going to spend a penny on investigating it. The study we do have is the only real indicator of the realities of this phenomenon. It found that 48 per cent of men who currently identify as gay had identified as bisexual at a previous point. A hefty 60.7 per cent said it was easier to think of themselves as bi than completely gay and 67.9 per cent thought others might have an easier time accepting them as bi than gay (Cox, 2018).

The most crucial finding of the report for me was the statistic that 82 per cent of the men who'd previously said they were bisexual didn't currently believe they actually were bisexual at that time. This is huge. It's one thing to think you might be bisexual on your journey of self-discovery, but for so many to use bisexuality in this way has had a negative impact.

The idea that a gay man who once identified as bi has any credibility to judge your sexuality is unfair. How can they say they know that our bisexuality isn't real if they were never actually bisexual themselves? They were scared gay men, hiding behind our label for protection. Just because they are happy and confident in who they are now, it doesn't mean they get to be the bully.

I usually end this point by saying that some gay men need to think about how they correct the damage they've inflicted on bi people. While we don't judge anyone for their coming-out journey, bisexual credibility has suffered because of gay men doing this.

Gay men who did use the bi label on their way out of the closet need to ask themselves how they are restoring the credibility of bisexuals. If all their friends and family see bisexuality as a phase of their coming-out journey, they do need to go back and clarify that bisexuality is a thing.

One of the areas where this issue is really big is in the world of celebrities. There are many celebrities, both men and women, who have publicly come out as bi, only to later come out as gay. While we won't name names, I have been shocked at how many of them have never publicly clarified that bisexuality was a valid orientation, just not one for them.

I've seen the real impact these events have on bi people. Some bisexuals get very excited when a celebrity they like comes out as bi. It's inspiring for them and makes them feel like they aren't alone. To then have that person come out as gay can be damaging, especially when that celebrity is used as proof that bisexuality is just a phase. I've personally experienced gay male celebrities being used as proof that my sexuality was a phase.

As we move forward, it is important that as bisexuals, while remaining compassionate, we call out this behaviour and force people to understand its impact. We won't be made fun of by gay men any more.

ADVICE FOR NON-BISEXUALS

Sometimes, it's not bisexuals who need answers – it's the people who encounter them. Some people find it hard to articulate how they feel; others can be scared to say anything for fear of being found offensive or insensitive. The following questions are for them.

How can I support my bi partner?

For many people dating someone bisexual, their minds will be drawn to how they can best support their partner. This again is an exercise of listening and understanding as every bi person is different. For some bi people, just you knowing and being supportive of them will be enough. Others might need you to talk through their issues with them and be a listening ear. Equally, some bi people will need to see that you have their back, ready to defend them when Auntie Nora makes a silly comment at the family barbecue.

You're also doing the right thing by reading a book like this one. Getting educated and listening to different perspectives on bisexuality will increase your understanding. I can't promise all bisexuals agree on everything, but that's part of the fun and gives you topics to discuss with your partner.

There is also a lot to be said for cheering your partner on – making them feel that you not only accept them but celebrate them for who they are. They'll love to see that you're their biggest champion and make them feel that their bisexuality is something you truly love about them. Letting them know you're proud of them and that their bisexuality is not just tolerated goes a long way and puts them at ease in the relationship.

It's also important to remember to be patient. Your partner might not know exactly how they feel about their bisexuality, they might not always be in the mood to talk about it and they might not have the answers to all the questions you have. Being understanding and allowing them to go at their own pace will serve you well.

Why does my partner need to make such a big deal out of being bi?

If you're in a relationship with a bi person, it can sometimes be difficult to understand why they keep talking about their bisexuality. You wouldn't like it if you were dating a straight woman and she kept talking about the men she was attracted to.

Motivations for bi people feeling the need to talk about their sexuality can differ, but one of the most common is the need to be visible. For too long, bisexuality has been seen as a phase: someone can be vocal about being bi when they are single, and then once they settle down, people think they have turned gay or straight. Talking about their bisexuality is the only tool they have for challenging this narrative. For some bisexuals, this is important as it took them so long and so much bravery to come out of the closet that they aren't going to be forced back in now.

For other bisexuals, being vocal about their bisexuality in a relationship is a way of giving back. When they were single, they didn't see other bisexuals in relationships. This meant they didn't get to see people like them enjoying their 'happily ever after' moment. It might have made them worry that bisexuals can't be in happy and fulfilling relationships. It also gives back by challenging the narrative that bisexuality is a phase. For them, being visible as bi in a relationship challenges the notion that you 'pick one eventually'. It's a way of inspiring younger bisexual people by showing the world that a relationship doesn't change your bisexuality.

It might make you uncomfortable, but the truth is this isn't about you; it's about your partner getting to be authentic, getting to be honest with the world about who they are and challenging any negative stereotypes around bisexuality. If you can, be supportive. Your partner has had a lifetime of dealing with the stigma around bisexuality. Maybe try to walk a mile in their shoes, tell your colleagues at work about your bi girlfriend and deal with any negative or ignorant comments. The ignorance your partner will have dealt with may have been hard and damaging to have experienced, and they are just trying to do what feels right for them. So, it's on you to figure out a way to support them in a way that feels right and authentic for you. You wouldn't want them to go back in the closet to make you happy, would you?

Should I let my bisexual teen have sleepovers?

An interesting question I've encountered over the years is 'Should a bi child be trusted to have sleepovers?' Typically, sleepovers at friends' houses have been determined by gender – a boys' night or a girls' night. But if your child is bi, they have the potential to be canoodling with either of these groups. Sometimes, parents don't know what to do for the best in this situation.

First, I'd point out that having gendered sleepovers is outdated; kids should know the rules, what's expected and any boundaries you've set. They should be allowed to invite people over regardless of their gender. It's about making sure you're having discussions and an open dialogue with your teenagers so they don't feel that sex, attraction and kissing are something taboo that they can't talk to you about.

With regard to bisexual teens, banning them from social events because of their sexuality is not the right thing to do. It's unfair and it's discrimination. It also won't help you in your quest to stop them from doing any kissing or sexual things with their friends. If two teenagers really want to kiss each other, they're going to find a way to do it. You can't be with them 24/7.

That's why the only option here is talking and trust. Make sure that you are there to guide them, not judge them, provide them with an adult perspective and keep them safe.

How do I deal with paranoia after my partner came out as bi?

For some people in relationships, their partner coming out as bi can be a challenging time. Am I enough? Will they cheat? Does everyone think I'm silly staying in this relationship? The paranoia can be a lot to handle.

The best thing to do if you're feeling this way is to dig your heels in. Don't let your partner's bisexuality become a taboo topic that is never discussed. Have an open dialogue and ask the questions you need to put your mind at ease. Find out who they are attracted to and find out about their libido. Use their coming out as an exercise in understanding your partner more deeply. By showing a willingness to understand, and by them opening up, you should arrive at a place where those negative voices in your head begin to quieten.

In truth, your partner's bisexuality doesn't put you at any more or less risk of being cheated on. Cheating is a personality trait, not a sexuality trait. Their coming out doesn't change things in a negative direction – on the contrary, it can bond you even more deeply.

At the end of the day, it all comes down to trust. Do you trust them? If not, then it's not healthy for either of you to stay in the relationship without such a fundamental component. To help with this, it might be an idea to call on your support network. Have trusted friends and family around you to talk through any fears or issues and let them help you understand your feelings and what is the right thing to do. Don't forget, there is also the option of seeking professional help. Therapists can be an important tool for helping you unlock your true feelings and working through your issues.

Also, spending time with your partner doing things you love is key. They aren't just bisexual; they are a whole person. Doing activities and spending time together doing the things you love and connecting can help you see that they haven't changed. They are still the same person you've always known; it's just that now you know a little bit more about them.

FINAL THOUGHTS

And here we are, at the end of the book. Make sure to post pictures on social media and push the book as much as possible. Not for my ego, but the more we prove there is money and interest in bisexuality, the more we'll be catered to.

Are there questions we haven't covered? Of course, no one book was going to have all the answers, but I hope I leave you in a more positive and empowered position than when you picked up this tome.

For those of you who maybe saw your bisexuality as an issue or a problem, I also hope that you've realized it is anything but – it's a superpower. One that needs training to handle, one that needs the experience of others to help you understand, but a superpower nonetheless. It opens up a world of possibilities that many don't get to experience, and embracing that path is far better than fighting it or, worse, apologizing for it. They say we only have one life, and you've been handed the bisexual card in yours, so wear it with pride. Enjoy the positive experiences it brings and use the tools this book has given you to quickly shut down any negative ones.

The world isn't perfect for bi people – that's why we need to be empowered. It's going to take you, me and as many bisexuals as possible to walk unapologetically and with confidence to shift the dial, so that, just maybe, the next generation doesn't have to deal with some of the negativity being bisexual brings. You're part of the solution. No matter how small or large your contribution to living proudly and publicly, it will shift people's perceptions. You can rewrite and rebrand bisexuality and make the world see what a gift it truly is. Bisexuality is a road less publicly travelled, which means you can write your own rules. So don't hide; get involved.

Bisexuality can help boost you in your relationships. Being able to understand both the male and female perspective means you can see beyond gender roles and think outside the box. You'll be able to better identify and understand what your partner needs from you and what you need from your partner.

Learning to accept your difference and walk with pride will likely make you less judgemental and more compassionate as a person. Bisexuals are different, but you'll notice that so is everyone else. Nobody is normal; everybody has something that's different about them. If you've learned to lean into your difference and celebrate that, others will want to be around you and be inspired by you, and it will help them on their journey of acceptance.

Bisexuality can also help you realize how grey and undefined most things are. Situations are rarely good or bad, black and white, and your bisexuality will not only help you notice that but also help you accept it. This can also help you in your relationships. Sometimes they will be undefined. Are you friends or more than that? Maybe you'll never have the answer, and that's okay. Bisexuals are better at living in the grey and not always needing everything labelled.

Acceptance as a bisexual will set you free and put you on a better path. Once you've had to fight to be who you are, you'll value yourself more. Being accepted wasn't just handed to you, so enjoy the good times when you have them, and remember that you are a fighter when you need to be.

Get out there, bisexuals, and own it!

References

Ballard, J. (2019) 'Millennials are more open to a bisexual partner than older generations – but not by much.' *YouGov*, 20 June. https://today. yougov.com/topics/society/articles-reports/2019/06/20/LGBTQ-dating-bisexual-trans-poll-2019

Bowen, A. (2012) 'Forty years of LGBTQ philanthropy 1970–2010.' *Funders for LGBTQ Issues*. https://lgbtfunders.org/wp-content/uploads/2018/04/40years_lgbtqphilanthrophy.pdf

Centers for Disease Control and Prevention (2010) 'NISVS: An overview of 2010 findings on victimization by sexual orientation.' The National Intimate Partner and Sexual Violence Survey (NISVS). www.cdc.gov/violenceprevention/pdf/cdc_nisvs_victimization_final-a.pdf

Columbia University Mailman School of Public Health (2013) 'Bisexual men on the "down low" run risk of poor mental health.' www.public health.columbia.edu/news/bisexual-men-down-low-run-risk-poor-mental-health

Cox, T. (2018) 'It's NOT just a phase! Tracey Cox reveals the six biggest myths about bisexuality – and, no, it doesn't mean you're more likely to cheat.' *MailOnline*, 31 October. www.dailymail.co.uk/femail/article-633 3871/Tracey-Cox-reveals-six-biggest-myths-bisexuality.html

GLAAD (2016) 'Reporting on the bisexual community: A resource for journalists and media professionals.' www.glaad.org/sites/default/files/BiMediaResourceGuide.pdf

Glass, K. (2018) 'Having it all: What is it like to be bisexual in 2018?' *The Times*, 16 December. www.thetimes.co.uk/magazine/the-sunday-times-magazine/having-it-all-what-is-it-like-to-be-bisexual-in-2018-zvxr759mj

Gleason, N., Vencill, J.A. and Sprankle, E. (2018) 'Swipe left on the bi guys: Examining attitudes toward dating and being sexual with bisexual individuals.' *Journal of Bisexuality 18*, 4, 516–534. https://doi.org/10.1080/15299716.2018.1563935

Hayes, K. (2016) 'Report shows STIs in gay and bisexual men on the rise.' *PinkNews*, 5 July. www.thepinknews.com/2016/07/05/report-shows-stis-in-gay-and-bisexual-men-on-the-rise

Jackman, J. (2017) 'Bisexual people are 80 percent more likely to feel anxiety than the average person.' *PinkNews*, 5 July. www.thepinknews.com/2017/07/05/bisexual-people-are-80-percent-more-likely-to-feel-anxiety-than-the-average-person

Kaplan, M. (2022) 'The more porn you watch, the more likely you are to be bisexual.' *New York Post*, 14 February. https://nypost.com/2019/02/26/people-who-watch-porn-are-more-likely-to-be-bisexual-study

Kristal, N. (2017) 'Bisexuals lack support – and it's literally killing us.' *HuffPost*, 5 April. www.huffpost.com/entry/bisexuals-lack-supportand_b_9585202

La Trobe University (2019) 'Study looks at bisexual mental health.' www.latrobe.edu.au/news/articles/2019/release/study-looks-at-bisexual-mental-health

Lawther, A., Wallace, A., Howe, E. and Frazer, S. (2022) '2019–2020 re-source tracking report: LGBTQ grantmaking by U.S. foundations.' *Funders for LGBTQ Issues*. https://lgbtfunders.org/wp-content/uploads/2022/06/2019-2020-Tracking-Report.pdf

Lees, E. (2016) 'Young gay and bisexual men more likely to attempt suicide.' *Counselling Directory*, 4 May. www.counselling-directory.org.uk/blog/2016/05/04/young-gay-bisexual-men

London Assembly Health Committee (2017) 'LGBT+ Mental Health.' www.london.gov.uk/sites/default/files/lgbtreportfinal.pdf

Metro Charity (2016) 'Youth Chances: Integrated Report.' https://metrocharity.org.uk/sites/default/files/2017-04/National%20Youth%20Chances%20Intergrated%20Report%202016.pdf

Perrie, S. (2021) 'People are fuming over the stat that 44% of Australians wouldn't date a bisexual person.' *LADbible*, 23 June. www.ladbible.com/news/latest-new-figures-reveal-44-of-australians-wouldnt-date-a-bisexual-person-20210623

Rankin, S., Morton, J. and Bell, M. (2015) 'Complicated? Bisexual People's Experiences of Mental Health and Support.' *Equality Network*. www.equality-network.org/wp-content/uploads/2015/04/Complicated-Bisexual-Report.pdf

Samuel, K. (2019) 'Marked changes in gay men's relationship agreements and condom use in the PrEP era.' *NAM AIDSmap*, 13 December. www.aidsmap.com/news/dec-2019/marked-changes-gay-mens-relationship-agreements-and-condom-use-prep-era

Taimi (2023) 'Not all unicorns and rainbows.' *Taimi*, 27 September. www.taimi.com/news/not-all-unicorns-and-rainbows

Tobkes, J.L. and Davidson, W.C. (2017) 'Over half of bisexual youth don't have family support.' *Psychology Today*, 14 October. www.psychologytoday.com/gb/blog/when-your-child-is-gay/201710/over-half-bisexual-youth-dont-have-family-support

Tsoulis-Reay, A. (2016) 'Are you straight, gay, or just...you?' *Glamour*, 11 February. www.glamour.com/story/glamour-sexuality-survey

Williams, J. (2016) 'Bisexual men make better lovers and fathers, study claims.' *PinkNews*, 5 September. www.thepinknews.com/2016/09/05/bisexual-men-make-better-lovers-and-father-study-claims